I Am My Beloved's

I Am My Beloved's

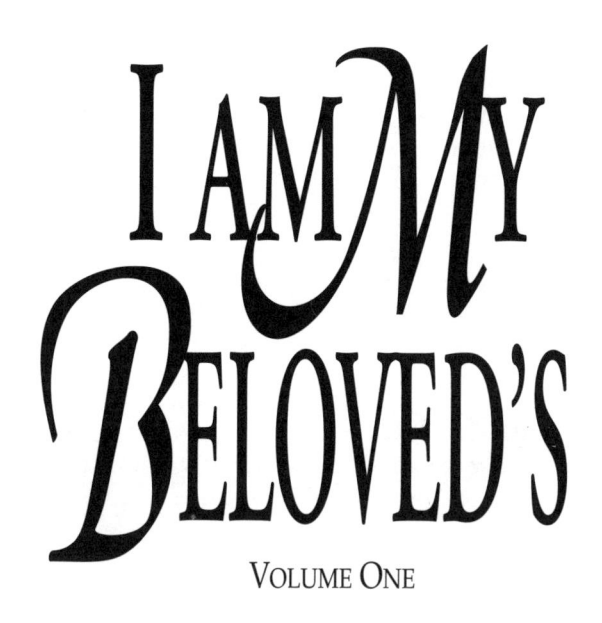

Volume One

JOHN W. BRAMHALL

GOSPEL FOLIO PRESS
P. O. Box 2041, Grand Rapids MI 49501-2041
Available in the UK from
JOHN RITCHIE LTD., Kilmarnock, Scotland

Originally published as regular correspondence to interested friends. Some letters have been previously published in *Counsel* magazine, *Uplook* magazine, and elsewhere.

Cover design by J. B. Nicholson, Jr.

Cover photo by Dan Spoelstra
Spoelstra Studios, Grand Rapids, Michigan

Copyright © 1994
Gospel Folio Press
All Rights Reserved

Published by Gospel Folio Press
P. O. Box 2041, Grand Rapids MI 49501-2041

ISBN 1-882701-10-0

Printed in the United States of America

*"The beloved of the Lord
shall dwell in safety by Him;
and the Lord shall cover him all the day long,
and he shall dwell between His shoulders."*

(Deuteronomy 33:12)

Contents

Foreword 9
Part One: Faith at Work 11
  1. Investing Your Life 13
  2. The Lord's People 17
  3. The Believer's Character & Conflict 21
  4. Faith Under Fire 25
  5. Danger Ahead 27
  6. Hold Fast 29
  7. Noble Ditchdiggers 33
  8. By Faith: Enoch's Homecoming 37
  9. Saints in Wrong Places 41
 10. Elijah's Last Journey 47
 11. The Blessings of Old Age 51
 12. God in the Stillness 55
 13. The Valley of the Shadow 59
Part Two: The Blessed Hope 63
 14. Crossroad of Eternity 65
 15. The Two Advents of Christ 69
 16. Are We Watching? 71
 17. The Morning Star 75
 18. What His Return Means to Me 79
 19. Raptured! 81

20. From Groans to Glory	87
21. Every Eye Shall See Him	91
22. The Last Wedding	95
23. Thy Kingdom Come	97
24. The Glories of Heaven	103
Part Three: Love's Sweet Secret	109
25. Three Great Landmarks of Love	111
26. The Direction of the Heart	115
27. John's School of Discipleship	117
28. Our Highest Occupation	119
29. The Bath, the Bason & the Bosom	121
Scripture Index	123

Foreword

The godly Adolph Saphir wrote: "In every age of the Church, the renewal of strength, the rekindling of love, the deliverance from languor and inertness bordering on death and destruction, can only proceed from a fuller and deeper knowledge of the Lord and His truth, from a renewed beholding of His countenance and glory.

"When the love of many shall wax cold, when iniquity shall abound...then let the Church...behold with open face the glory of Christ; and gazing on His brightness, she will be strong and courageous, and remain steadfast unto the end."

Now we have reached that time which, for the Church, is characterized by love waxed cold, power diminished, and a creeping sloth that settles for carnal alternatives, soulish excitement, and worldly methods. If ever we needed a "renewed beholding of His countenance and glory" it is in this day, and every day until we behold our beloved Lord "without a cloud between."

This is what John Bramhall's ministry is all about. It is directed to the turning of our hearts and our vision to renewed occupation with Christ.

These papers, now in this more permanent form, were first mailed as letters to friends and neighbors. Then many of them appeared in magazine form to bless a wider audience of readers around the world.

This is not a collection of mystical meanderings, but clear, simple, and inspiring expositions of Scripture. Word portraits of our beloved Lord capture our attention. Calls to faithful and holy living claim our response. The balm of divine consolations comforts our hearts, and fingerposts point to the soon coming One to strengthen our faith and inspire our hope.

These papers are a distillation of a long life lived for God, not secluded in some comfortable cloister, but in the vicissitudes of life "through the waters...through the rivers...through the fire."

These papers will touch the heart that hungers for God. They will call the weary feet to the high road that marks out the "heavenly places in Christ" and bring the "oil of consolation" to those who are weary of the world's false ways, and tired of the froth and frivolity of religious entertainment.

It has been this writer's privilege to have known Mr. Bramhall for many years, to have relished his Christ-exalting ministry, and to have fellowshipped with him in the royal service of the Best of Masters. As editor of *Counsel* magazine, I have been happy to include many of his papers for the blessing of readers in more than ninety countries.

As the reader takes up this volume, I can think of no better counsel than that expressed by the hymn:

> *"Turn your eyes upon Jesus,*
> *Look full in His wonderful face,*
> *And the things of earth*
> *Will grow strangely dim,*
> *In the light of His glory and grace."*

J. BOYD NICHOLSON, SR.
St. Catharines, Ontario

Part One
Faith at Work

1
Investing Your Life

Over the triple doorways of Milan Cathedral there are three inscriptions spanning the arches. Above one is carved a wreath of roses and underneath is the legend: "All that pleases is but for a moment." Over the second is sculptured a cross, and underneath are the words: "All that troubles is but for a moment." Above the great central entrance to the main aisle of the cathedral is the inscription: "That only is important which is eternal." The brevity of life in contrast to permanent value of eternal things should be constantly realized. The Bible states:

Life is a tale: "We spend our years as a tale that is told" (Ps. 90:9). It does not take long to spin a tale, and the end of the story arrives. Such is our brief life. The Hebrew rendering could read: "We spend our years as a passing thought" (New Trans., JND). It may be many years to us, but in contrast to eternity, it is only "a passing thought." How brief!

Life is a pilgrimage: "For we are strangers before Thee, and sojourners, as were all our fathers; our days on earth are as a shadow, and there is none abiding" (1 Chron. 29:15). Our life here is a short journey; a brief pilgrimage through this world. Like a moving shadow that quietly flits across the sands of time, we hardly see it go. Every sunset sees us closer Home.

Life is just a handbreadth: "Behold, Thou hast made my days as an handbreadth, and mine age is as nothing before Thee" (Ps. 39:5). God quickly answered David's desire "to know the measure" of his days (Ps. 39:4). Contrasted to eternity, our lives measure the width of a hand! But contrasted to the Eternal One, they are "as nothing!" With what grace, then, God came to dwell in time with His creatures. Emmanuel!

Life is like a vapor: "For what is your life? It is even a vapor, that appeareth for a little time, and then vanisheth away" (Jas. 4:14). Not that brief, you say? That is what God says it is in relation to eternity. The next opportunity you have, watch the rising of vapor and its quick disappearance from sight. This is your life. You do not have long to live it.

Life is like a flower: "Man that is born of a woman is of few days, and full of trouble. He cometh forth like a flower, and is cut down" (Job. 14:1-2). Brief, but troubled, was Job's comment of life and often this is our judgment, too. Like a flower, now budding, then blooming, but suddenly gone. "Cut down." It matters not which flower you may think you are like (from a roadside daisy to a hothouse orchid), "the flower" we cherish, nourish, and admire is soon gone. What fragrance will linger after you are gone?

Life is but a tent: "For we who are in this tent sigh under our burden" (2 Cor. 5:4, Confraternity). Note the context of this chapter from verse 1, and realize that your body and mine is no more than a temporary dwelling for the spirit and soul, just a tent. Nothing permanent about that! A vulnerable structure that soon shows signs of wear and tear from the experiences of life. The believer's permanent "house from heaven" is eternal, a new body of glory, but this present one is only a tent, patches and all. It barely survives life's storms and will soon be taken down.

Life is as grass: "All flesh is grass, and all the goodliness thereof is as the flower of the field: the grass withereth, the flower fadeth: because the spirit of the Lord bloweth upon it: surely the people is grass" (Isa. 40:6-7). The scorching sun and the cold of winter both blight the tender grass, withering it away. How quickly it is destroyed. Everything may look green in life, but one blast from the breath of God can soon take it all away. How uncertain life is and how brief. It is sown, blown, mown—and gone!

Thus the Holy Scriptures vividly and accurately describe the brevity of life in contrast to eternity and the One who is Eternal. Let us acknowledge the truth of God's Word with a deeper realization of life's brevity compared with eternity.

The application of these truths should be realized and the lessons taught us assimilated into our hearts. The inscriptions over the triple doorways of Milan Cathedral are amplified by the scriptures to which we referred:

a) "All that pleases is but for a moment." Living for the pleasures of this life alone, carelessly indifferent to eternal things, can be disastrous and wasteful. All that the world holds for the gratifying of human pleasure is but a momentary object. The world congratulates you on your achievement of wealth and honor, if you live for self. Not so your Saviour! "For whosoever shall desire to save his life shall lose it" (Mk. 8:35, New Trans.) The world condemns and reproaches you if you live for eternity and value eternal things. Not so your Saviour! "Whosoever shall lose his life for My sake and the gospel's, the same shall save it (Mk. 8:35). Which world are you living for, this or the next? Life is short for us. Are we really losing or saving it?

b) "All that troubles is but for a moment." Not only should the pleasures of life be realized as a momentary object, but also our troubles. Often we may unduly magnify them, but we should not. Compared with eternity and eternal glory, God says they are a momentary experience: "our light affliction, which is but for a moment" (2 Cor. 4:17). The inscription over the cathedral door is scriptural truth. The brevity of life, contrasted with eternity, should enable us to minimize our troubles for the glory of God.

c) "That only is important which is eternal." Here the proper emphasis on our life is rightly placed. This is a divine encouragement to us. Read carefully the context of 2 Corinthians 4:15-18. There you will find the true perspective on life revealed. Part of it reads as follows: "Our light affliction, which is but for a moment, worketh for us a far more exceeding and eternal weight of glory; while we look not at the things which are seen, but at the things which are not seen: for the things which are seen are temporal; but the things which are not seen are eternal."

What a lesson in contrasts: "a light affliction" and "weight of glory." One is "for a moment" and the other is "eternal." One is "light" and the other "exceeding heavy." Note the contrasts between "the things that are seen" and "the things that are not seen." The former are temporal and the latter are eternal. The old brother was not far from the truth when he deliberated over his troubles in life and said he was truly thankful for the oft repeated phrase in the Word of God, "And it came to pass…" He realized that his troubles had not come to stay. It was a good way of looking at "bad" events in life, something we need to remember.

So in your pathway and mine, in this brief life, which "things" are our hearts centered on—the "temporal" or the "eternal"? The brevity of life should stimulate us to live for eternal glory rather than earthly things. Let us permit the Spirit of God to inscribe deeply into our lives the blessed truth: "that only is important which is eternal."

> *"Take my life and let it be*
> *Consecrated, Lord, to Thee;*
> *Take myself and I will be*
> *Ever, only, all for Thee."*

2
The Lord's People

One of the great joys of David's life was the momentous occasion when the Ark of God was brought to its sweet resting place in Jerusalem. It inspired a song of thanksgiving from the heart of the sweet singer of Israel as the city reverberated with holy joy. Toward the end of the song, David described four features that are to characterize God's people at all times, saying, "And, say ye, Save us, O God of our salvation, and gather us together, and deliver us from the heathen, that we may give thanks to Thy holy name, and glory in Thy praise" (1 Chron. 16:35).

SALVATION

This is the first characteristic of God's beloved people: "Say ye, Save us, O God of our salvation." We are a saved people! Salvation is the foundation of everything to us, for time and eternity. Salvation is a word of broad meaning in Scripture, but let us consider that God's salvation is a deliverance from every peril that could threaten us, whether in the past, present, or future:

1. Our past deliverance is by the death of Christ. When we trusted Christ and His finished work on the Cross, that moment the sins of the past were forgiven. Our penalty—death—(Rom. 6:23) was forever removed (Jn. 5:24); our fear of hell was gone (Ps. 40:3), and the guilty conscience was purged (Heb. 9:14). We now look back to Calvary by faith, and through His death can say, we *have been* saved.

2. Our present deliverance is by the priesthood of Christ.

Salvation also means the deliverance from the present dangers in this world. We daily need to be saved from our enemies—the world, the flesh, and the devil. But how? There are three sources of help. First, "we have a great High Priest" in heaven above, who by His present intercessory work succors us (Heb. 2:18; 4:14-16; 7:25). Second, we have the Holy Spirit of God, our indwelling Comforter within our hearts (Rom. 8). Third, we have the Word of God, the comfort of the Scriptures (Ps. 119:11; Rom. 15:4; 2 Tim. 3:14-17). Thus our God, through the priesthood of Christ, the ministry of the Spirit, and the influence of the Word, has provided us with present power for deliverance in this world. We *are being* saved.

3. Our future deliverance is by the coming of Christ. Blessed be His name! Our complete deliverance will be effected, "spirit, soul and body," at His return. Surely it is a blessed hope that is ours! (Rom. 8:23-25; Phil. 3:20, 21; 1 Pet. 1:3-5). We *shall be* saved.

ASSOCIATION

This is the second characteristic feature of the Lord's people: "and gather us together." We are "called out" of this world. However, it is not for isolation but for holy association that our God has sent the Holy Spirit from heaven, that His people may be gathered "together," forming the Body of Christ.

1. The Body of Christ is a heavenly association formed by the Spirit of God at Pentecost, eternally uniting every believer with Christ, the Head, in heaven and also bringing into union every member (1 Cor. 12:13; Eph. 1:22-23; 2:10; 5:30). May God keep before us this precious truth that we are in association with all believers, a bond formed by the Spirit of God.

2. The Cross is the foundation of this heavenly people. It is through the work of Christ at Calvary that God has thus made the "one new man" (Eph. 2:13-16). How expensive!

3. God tells us how to maintain this fellowship with Him and with one another, if we will obey His Word—in the sevenfold spirit of lowliness, meekness, longsuffering, forbearance, love, diligence, and peace (Eph. 4:3-6).

In these days of divided and darkened Christendom, may the Spirit of God help us to be faithfully associated "with them that call on the Lord out of a pure heart" (2 Tim. 2:22), seeking to maintain by His grace a practical expression of the truth of the Body of Christ, no matter how outwardly feeble the effort may seem.

SEPARATION

Here is the third characteristic feature of the Lord's beloved people: "deliver us from the heathen." God's protection for Israel depended solely on their unlikeness and separation *from* the nations around them; never upon their federation *with* them. This same principle is to govern us today as His people; a separation manifested in a twofold way to have proper balance:

1. There is separation *from:* "unrighteousness, darkness, flesh, infidelity," etc.,—all moral evil and all unequal yokes (2 Cor. 6:14-17; 2 Tim. 2:20-21). Though we are in the world, we should not be of it (Jn. 17:15-17), and by the Spirit of God's guidance and the bright light of the Word, we should be free from all moral and doctrinal evil.

2. There is a separation *unto*—a positive emphasis on separation truth! We are to be separate unto "the Father," to be "perfecting holiness in the fear of God"; to enjoy "the love of the Father" (2 Cor. 6:18 to 7:1; 1 Jn. 2:15-17). We are separated unto "Jesus also" that we may take our place with Him in this rejected world, "Let us go forth therefore unto Him without the camp, bearing His reproach" (Heb. 13:12-13).

Surely our separation should have the testimony of this twofold character for us to maintain a scriptural testimony for the glory of God!

ADORATION

This is the final characteristic feature of the Lord's beloved people mentioned in 1 Chronicles 16:35, "that we may give thanks to Thy holy name and glory in Thy praise." God's purpose and desire for us is to make us a worshipping people, offering "the sacrifice of praise to God continually, that is, the fruit of our lips, giving thanks to His Name" (Heb. 13:15).

The essential feature of Christian worship is that we worship "the Father." Said the Lord Jesus, "The true worshippers shall worship the Father in spirit and in truth; for the Father seeketh such to worship Him" (Jn. 4:23). God is known by us as Father through His beloved Son. Our hearts, in the joy of our salvation, association, and separation should be crying out, "Abba, Father, we adore thee!" (Gal. 4:6). This is the divine objective in the purposes of God in saving us, gathering us and separating us, that through endless ages with Himself we shall fill the universe to come with our endless praises unto the Father (Ps. 84:4).

> "Rise our hearts, and bless the Father.
> Ceaseless song e'en here begun,
> Endless praise and adoration
> To the Father and the Son."

May God the Holy Spirit, as we yield to Him, manifest these marks of divine glory upon our features even now, for His name's sake.

3
The Believer's Character & Conflict

The definition of character has been stated as "the stamp of the individual; the mental and moral qualities" (A.T. Schofield). The same writer adds, "The spring or sources of character are the instincts of heredity in the unconscious mind, supplemented by others acquired during life through habit." Though true, yet the believer must realize that spiritual character is produced in him, not by self, but by the Spirit of God. He alone can reproduce the character of Christ in us.

TWO ALTERNATIVES FOR THE BELIEVER

The believer has the alternative of either of two principles of life: a carnal walk in the energy of the flesh—"as men," or a spiritual walk by the energy of the Spirit of God—"as Christ." It is impossible to live according to both principles. "The flesh" and "the Spirit" are opposed to each other (Gal. 5:17).

God commands us to "walk in the Spirit" (Gal. 5:16). This demands our yielding to the Spirit of God, that a spiritual character may be formed in us according to His will (Rom. 12:1-2). Can we refuse to choose this path? God forbid! The desire of "the new man" is: "For to me to live is Christ" (Phil. 1:21). Complete submission to the Spirit of God will enable the features of Christ to be reproduced in us.

THE FRAGRANCE OF SPIRITUAL CHARACTER

Spiritual character is the presence of divine characteristics in the life, a fragrance expected by God and produced by His

Spirit. In Galatians 5:22-23, it is revealed as beautiful fruit: "the fruit (not fruits) of the Spirit." Nine fragrant graces of Christ are described, each one exalting a particular virtue of His Person. Gaze upon them with an aspiring heart, meditating prayerfully on each one:

Love: Does His love pour through your heart? (Rom. 5:5); *Joy:* Are you filled with His joy? (Jn. 15:11); *Peace:* Do you have an untroubled heart? (Jn. 14:27); *Longsuffering:* How much patience have you under fire? (Jas. 5:7-11; 1 Cor. 13:4); *Kindness:* Are you gentle and kind? (Eph. 4:32); *Goodness:* Are you doing good? (Acts 10:38; Gal. 6:10); *Faith [or fidelity]:* Are you dependable? (1 Cor. 4:2, 17); *Meekness:* Are you puffed up? (1 Cor. 13:4); Or like Moses? (Num. 12:3); Or better still, like your Saviour? (Isa. 53:7; 1 Pet. 2:23); *Temperance:* Are self and the flesh in complete subjection? (1 Cor. 9:25-27).

THE REWARD OF SPIRITUAL CHARACTER

First, there is a present reward. The Father rejoices to see the character of His Son in us (1 Pet. 1:14-16). Those who are with us also will see the features of Christ as they watch our lives (2 Cor. 3:2-3). Could we have a greater testimony in this life? Never!

Second, there is a future reward. Have you realized that each believer, at the Judgment Seat of Christ (2 Cor. 5:10), will be "manifested"? This means that our true character will be displayed before all. All pretense gone forever! We shall be revealed exactly as God sees us. What we are (not our reputation) will be revealed. Would you not like a fully developed spiritual character to be seen in that day? Surely you would. Then go after this, beloved. Yield yourselves to the Spirit of God. It is of eternal value. All your earthly possessions will be left here, but your character you will take with you into eternity.

OUR SPIRITUAL BLESSINGS

The possessions of a Christian are declared in Ephesians 1:3. He is "blessed…with all spiritual blessings in heavenly places in Christ." The present enjoyment of these blessings can be greatly affected by Satan and his evil hosts. The enemy is ceaseless in his effort to prevent the spiritual education and development of the Christian in the things of God while passing through this world.

OUR SPIRITUAL ENEMIES

The character of the enemy should be known by the believer. First, we do not struggle "against flesh and blood," though such may be used as instruments by the foe (Eph. 6:12). Second, the Spirit describes our enemies as principalities, authorities, universal lords of darkness, spiritual powers of wickedness in the heavenlies (Eph. 6:12; Eph. 2:2). Once we were under their authority, but since giving our allegiance to Christ, they are against us with a vengeance! It is their grand purpose to keep us from being transformed to be like Christ; their diabolical intent is to conform us to this world.

OUR SPIRITUAL PROVISION

For the conflict, God has faithfully provided divine armor. It is "powerful through God to the pulling down of strongholds" but not in any way of "fleshy"origin (see 2 Cor. 10:3-5). The flesh is completely impotent, and only in the energy of the Spirit of God can we defeat the foe. In the context of Ephesians 6:10-18, the armor is described as being "of God." This will prove invincible against the enemy when we have it on. It consists of seven parts, five that are defensive in character and two that are offensive. Consider them prayerfully:

The Secret Strength of the Inner Life: "Having your loins girt about with truth." In Roman warfare, a belt encircled the loins of the soldier. This is symbolic of our unseen spiritual strength, the truth of God controlling and motivating the heart and life of the Christian. Obedience to God's Word leads to victory against Satan. Read the best example of this in Luke 4:1-13. If your belt is loose, better tighten it!

The Outward Testimony of Righteousness: "Having on the breastplate of righteousness." Here is an outward evidence of true Christian living, being "an example of the believers, in word, in conduct, in love, in faith, in purity" (1 Tim. 4:12). Wear your breastplate; polish it brightly if it's a bit rusty! As John reminds us: Don't let anyone fool you. If you do what is right, you are right; if you don't do what is right, you are not right. No amount of rationalization will change that.

The Continual Enjoyment of God's Peace: "Your feet shod with the preparation of the Gospel of peace." To stand our ground against the foe, we need these shoes. The gospel brought us peace—"peace with God" and "the peace of God." No matter the troubles, we should enjoy this peace, His peace. (See Jn. 14:27; Isa. 26:3; Phil. 4:6-7). Be sure to keep your shoes on. Don't be found barefoot!

The Implicit Confidence of Faith: "Above all, the shield of faith." Fiery darts of doubt, despair, and discouragement are hurled against us by the foe to make us distrust God. Use your shield! Trust Him in the darkness as well as in the sunlight (Prov. 3:5-6).

The Intelligence of Salvation: "And take the helmet of salvation." Don't be weak in the head. The head is the seat of intelligence, and every Christian should have a complete knowledge of all that salvation means: past, present, and future. Make sure you know what your salvation is, and don't lose your head in this place of the battle! Many have and are uncertain of their salvation. Be an intelligent Christian as well as an affectionate one!

The Sword of the Spirit: "Which is the Word of God." This is the first offensive weapon. Jesus proved it as a Man and "the devil left Him" (Lk. 4:13). We can use it, too. It is the most powerful weapon against spiritual enemies. Read Hebrews 4:12 and make sure you have a firm grip on this Sword. It must be used by the Spirit of God through you. It is not called your sword, but "the Sword of the Spirit." A carnal Christian cannot use it properly; only a spiritual one can. Use it like Eleazar (2 Sam. 23:10). But practice your swordsmanship before the crisis comes.

Continual Dependence on God: "Praying always with all prayer." This is essential for every part of the armor. "Each piece put on with prayer," says the songwriter. Perpetual dependence on God is the only safe condition for the spiritual man, for prayer is all-important: Don't stop praying!

Then will be fulfilled John's words, "The wicked one does not touch him" (1 Jn. 5:18). May God help us to be victorious in our daily conflict and see each sunset bringing us a little closer to conformity to Christ.

4
Faith Under Fire

As you read the prophecy of Habakkuk, you notice the message of each chapter.

In Chapter 1, it is *the trial of faith*. The prophet pours out his grief before the Lord: "O Lord, how long shall I cry, and Thou wilt not hear?" (vv. 2-4). He sorrowed over the tragic conditions in Israel and the seeming silence of God. God answers in verses 5-11 and announces coming judgment at the hands of the Chaldeans, His chastening instruments.

Shocked and grieved, yet knowing the everlasting God was a covenant-keeping God, the prophet pleads for Him not to destroy His people and neither remain silent towards the oppressors: "Wherefore lookest Thou upon them that deal treacherously, and holdest Thy tongue?" (vv. 12-17). Are we to be oppressed continually? he wonders.

Chapter 2 gives us *the vision of faith*. Habakkuk waits, saying, "I will stand upon my watch, and set me upon the tower, and will watch to see what He will say unto me, and what I shall answer when I am reproved" (v. 1). What a blessed attitude of waiting on God and for God! The answer comes in verses 2 to 4. God gives him a vision. It is the appearing of our great God and Saviour, Jesus Christ (Titus 2:13), when He shall establish His millennial kingdom of glory on the earth. The apostle confirms this fact in Hebrews 10:37. The words of the prophet in verse 14 refer to that kingdom of glory on the earth.

Note the purpose of the vision: "that he may run that readeth it." Here is spiritual progress. Notice also the certainty of it: "an appointed time." In God's schedule "it shall surely come." But faith is required to enter into the good of it: "the just shall live by his faith" (v. 4) for faith rests on the promises of God, making the vision real to the soul while waiting for it. (See Heb. 11:1.) The rest of the chapter reveals God's destruction of the nations who seek to destroy His people. At the final deliverance of Israel, it will be fulfilled that "the Lord is in His holy temple, let all the earth keep silence before Him" (v. 20).

Chapter 3 presents us with *the triumph of faith.* As he hears of coming judgment, the prophet prays for revival, yet requests of God, "in wrath remember mercy." When God's wrath falls on the world in that day of universal judgment, He will remember mercy, according to the words of Revelation 7.

Then in our chapter follows a vivid description in verses 3 to 15 of the second coming of Christ to the earth in power and judgment. It will be judgment on unbelieving Gentiles and apostate Jews alike, but deliverance for the believing remnant of that day. This description produces fear and trembling to the prophet, for it is "that great and terrible day of the Lord" (Acts 2:30). The prophet prays for "rest in the day of trouble."

Then follows *his song of faith* in verses 17-19. Note the two words, "although" and "yet." No matter how fiery the trials, faith triumphantly sings: "I will rejoice in the Lord, I will joy in the God of my salvation." Why? "Because He will surely come, He will not tarry" (Hab. 2:3, Septuagint). The triumph of faith in the midst of our circumstances rests on the vision of faith, the personal return of our Lord. The prophet begins his prophecy with a sigh but ends it with a song. It is a song that reaches to the "high places." His song of faith reaches the "chief singer" above, even our Lord Jesus Christ. Surely in the midst of earth's trials today, the believer should learn to sing this triumphant victory song of faith.

> *"Then joy unmingled will be thine,*
> *Earth's tears and trials all forgot:*
> *So cheer thy heart, no more repine,*
> *His Word is sure; He'll tarry not!"*

5
Danger Ahead

A frequent word in the New Testament is "faith," but it has two meanings: 1) In a subjective sense, it is the act of believing. 2) In an objective sense, it is what is believed (see Jude 3). This is the doctrine taught as the truth of God. A series of warnings are found in 1 Timothy regarding various ways by which men depart from the truth. Beware the paths that lead away from the faith!

In the personal life (1 Tim. 1:19). Some having put away a good conscience made shipwreck of the faith. The first sign of departure from "the faith" can be a personal and inward failure, the commencement of all failure. Compare 1 Timothy 1:20 with 2 Timothy 2:17-18, concerning Hymeneus who trifled with his conscience, wrecked his own testimony, and many others, by his teaching. How important to keep a tender conscience.

In the assembly life (1 Tim. 4:1). Some giving heed to seducing spirits, and teaching of demons, shall depart (apostatize) from the faith. This is the worst and most dangerous, for it is a deliberate act by Satan. Compare 1 Timothy 3:15-16 and see the connection—God's doctrine concerning His Son, versus the doctrine of demons. Here are two opposing forces: the testimony of God and the testimony of Satan "speaking lies." They are new rules and new teachings which may appear of little importance, but which Satan uses to ultimately produce departure from the truth, undermining the truth and scattering the saints. This is a very present danger.

In the domestic life (1 Tim. 5:8). "If any provide not for his own,

...he hath denied the faith." We can drive others from the truth by our own bad testimony at home, though we may not be in danger of turning from it ourselves. Last day perils in 2 Timothy 3:1-5 include being "without natural affection" and children "disobedient to parents." If Christian parents do not control themselves, they will not turn their children to the Lord. Christian children who do not honor their parents are also a bad testimony. Watch the home life!

In the social life (1 Tim. 5:11-15). Note verse 12, "They have cast off their first faith," and verse 15, "for some are already turned aside after Satan." Some women, by careless conduct and speech, turned aside after Satan in social contacts, "wandering about from house to house." The social life is a constant danger for believers.

In the business life (1 Tim. 6:9-10). "For the love of money is the root of all evil, which while some coveted after, they have erred (strayed) from the faith." The coveting of riches is a snare! The willfulness to be rich can lead away from the Christian faith and produce pain and sorrow. Note Psalm 62:10. When the heart covets riches, that is a "snare" that can pull the believer "from the faith." Watch it!

In the intellectual life (1 Tim. 6:20-21). "Avoiding profane, vain babblings, and opposition of false-named knowledge, of which some, having made a profession, have missed the faith" (JND Trans.). Some, professing superior knowledge that is false, miss the mark entirely concerning the faith! We must hold fast to the truth of God. Humanistic philosophies and "science falsely so-called" that is contrary to the Word of God, if followed, will lead away from the faith. "The world by wisdom knew not God" writes the Spirit of God in 1 Corinthians 1:21. Sanctified knowledge can be used by God, but must conform to the truth of God.

When the apostle wrote these warnings, the dangers were real, not imaginary. Into most of them "some" had already fallen and into others "some" were going to fall sooner or later. These dangers are more apparent today than when Paul wrote them. Is not the exhortation appropriate for us? "Wherefore let him that thinketh he standeth take heed lest he fall" (1 Cor. 10:12).

6
Hold Fast

A spiritual disease of Latitudinarianism prevails among the saints today, even among those who in the past have maintained the truth of God. This name emerged in the 17th and 18th Centuries within the Church of England, when certain religious leaders tended to minimize Christian doctrines. Its continuance to the 19th Century produced a liberal theology. Following it, the Spirit of God manifested the greatest revival of divine truth ever known since the early history of the church.

Webster's dictionary defines *Latitudinarianism* as "deviations from a standard of belief and opinion, especially in matters of religion; tolerant of deviation in opinion and doctrine." A person who is a "latitudinarian," the same source describes such as "one who is broad and liberal in his standard of belief and conduct." William Kelly, in his exposition of Revelation, describes this as Laodicean in character: "'I know thy works, that thou art neither cold nor hot.' This is Latitudinarianism. It is not ignorance that works the deadly mischief, but the heart remaining indifferent to the truth, after it has fully been brought before it."

The apostle Paul admonished Timothy, "Hold fast the form of sound words" (2 Tim. 1:13). The spirit of indifference to Pauline truth is in strong evidence today. One has said, "Evangelicalism without being followed by teaching will lead to the abandonment of Pauline truth" (J. N. Darby). Let us analyze the words of 2 Timothy 1:13.

What to do: "Hold fast." The truth of God is to be firmly held. "Buy the truth, and sell it not" (Prov. 23:23). There is always someone else bidding for it against the Lord's people—the devil!

What to hold: "The form of sound words." We quote from the footnote of JND's Translation: "Timothy had heard words or doctrines. Hence he was to have a summary or outline, so as to state clearly and definitely what he did hold."

What are sound words? The word "sound" is linked with doctrine four times (in 1 Tim. 1:10; 2 Tim. 4:3; Titus 1:9; Titus 2:1). It is also linked with "words" two times (1 Tim. 6:3, "wholesome words; 2 Tim. 1:13). It is also linked with "in the faith" in Titus 1:13 and 2:2. The word "sound" is a semi-medical one, referring to the spiritual health of the believer. Health-giving teaching is to produce healthy saints. The remedy for the absence of spiritual growth is to be the medicine of healthy teaching.

What is the source of sound words? "Which thou hast heard of me," writes Paul. If Paul could speak today regarding church conditions, would he not quote his own words in Acts 27:21? Eliminate the Pauline epistles and spiritual tragedy follows in the testimony. Under God, we are indebted to His servant Paul for church guidance in truth and practice. Through him God completed the divine revelation of truth (see Col. 1:25-28), the mystery of the Church!

What is the evidence of sound words? It is possible to hold sound doctrine and still remain in an unhealthy state of soul. The genuine proof is when it is assimilated into personal experience. In 2 Timothy 1:12, the effective experience of practiced truth in Paul's life is recorded (also in 2 Tim. 3:10-12). You find in the pastoral letters two great principles emphasized: sound doctrine and sound living. Paul could never be accused of "mentally trafficking in unfelt truth" as some of our preachers of the past often said. His life supported his admonition to Timothy to "hold fast" in the midst of departure from the truth that had already set in, many having defected (2 Tim. 1:15). If Timothy faced this danger in his day, what shall we say of it now?

The danger of being like so much dead driftwood and carried about by winds of doctrine and waves of circumstances is strong today (Eph. 4:14-15). Hence the importance of faithfulness to God's Word and constant spiritual growth. In relation to the truth of God, in 2 Timothy we are admonished to hold it (2 Tim

1:13); to teach it (2 Tim. 2:2); to abide in it (2 Tim. 3:14); and to preach it (2 Tim. 4:2). Let us search our hearts and ask: "Am I heeding Paul's admonition to hold fast?" Or am I a Latitudinarian?

In these days of spiritual declension, this exhortation is necessary. The phrase "hold fast" occurs twelve times in Scripture, for however dark and how difficult the path, we ought to have a strong grip on God's truth. If we are inclined to let it go, we should repent and tighten our grip. Consider some important truths we should "hold fast."

1. *The gospel* (1 Cor. 15:1-4). Paul delighted in the declaration of the gospel, which we have believed and by which we are saved. Many preach on moral problems, current questions, and give sermonettes on topics innumerable, instead of preaching the "death, burial and the resurrection" of Christ as the message of salvation. All need to hear the glorious tidings in simplicity and power (note Gal. 1:9). Let us hold fast the gospel.

2. *Assurance of salvation* (Jn. 3:36; 5:24; 1 Jn. 5:13; 2 Tim. 1:12). Take God at His word. The believer is not only saved but safe! He can "never perish" (Jn. 10:28, etc.). The Scripture was given "that ye may know that ye have eternal life." How unfortunate that so many believers think their salvation can be lost. You cannot lose anything God gives that is eternal. Let us hold fast to our blessed assurance.

3. *Inspiration of the Scriptures* (2 Tim. 3:16-17; 2 Pet. 1:21). Probably the longest and greatest theological battle rages over the fallibility or infallibility of the Bible. Prominent ecclesiastical leaders openly deny the verbal inspiration of the Bible in its inerrancy. Yet godly men in the past century whose hearts the Lord touched, after much prayer and study of God's Word, repudiated all creeds, catechisms, and confessions, and took the Bible for their complete guide in all matters relating to the Church and Christian life. The Bible stands; hold it fast.

4. *The gathering name of Christ* (Mt. 18:20). One precious Name alone expresses the unity of the Church. "My name," said the Lord Jesus! Paul stated it in 1 Corinthians 1:2, yet even in his day some were not satisfied with this (see 1 Cor. 1:12). The only church which Scripture gives us authority to belong to, is called

the church of the living God (1 Tim. 3:15). All true believers are in this "Body of Christ" (1 Cor. 12:13) and united to the risen Head in heaven (Eph. 1:22-23). If you are one, practice this truth and hold it fast.

5. *The priesthood of all believers* (1 Pet. 2:1-10). Note we are a "holy priesthood" and a "royal priesthood" (vv. 5, 9). Every believer, young or old, is a priest in God's spiritual house. There are no distinctions—such as clergy or laity—for each one is called and ordained by God to enjoy immediate access into God's presence at all times and in all circumstances (Heb. 10:19). We may have different functions to perform as God reveals, but we are equally the same in the priesthood (read Rev. 1:5-6; 5:10). How precious to recognize the whole priesthood is under the authority of the great High Priest above (Heb. 4:14-16; 7:25). Hold it fast!

6. *Separation to God* (2 Cor. 6:14-18). In the spiritual realm we are to walk separate from the world (Jn. 15:19; 1 Jn. 2:15). We are to be separate from the "disorderly" (2 Thess. 3:6); separate from those with unsound doctrine (2 Jn. 8-10); and from immorality (1 Cor. 5:11, 13). But above all, we are to be separated unto God. Remember that separation from true believers, sound in faith and godly in life, is not taught in the New Testament. God's children are to be a separated people, not from each other but from those influences that would keep us from each other! This is greatly neglected. We need to hold it fast.

7. *The coming of the Lord* (Jn. 14:1-3; Acts 1:11; 1 Thess. 4:13-18; 1 Cor. 15:51-54). The pre-millennial return of the Saviour is our blessed hope. This doctrine has been abused and emasculated by some, bringing confusion to many saints. But let us be "looking for that blessed hope and the glorious appearing of the great God and our Saviour, Jesus Christ (Titus 2:13). Keep saying: "Even so, come, Lord Jesus." And in the meantime, hold fast!

7
Noble Ditchdiggers

In Numbers 21:16-18, we read, "And from thence they went to Beer; that is the well whereof the Lord spake unto Moses, Gather the people together, and I will give them water. Then Israel sang this song: Spring up, O well; sing ye unto it; the princes digged the well, the nobles of the people digged it, by the direction of the lawgiver, with their staves."

Every Bible reader is acquainted with the fact that the forty years of wilderness wanderings in Israel, has a present application for the people of God today as we journey through this world. According to 1 Corinthians 10:11, these Old Testament experiences have much to teach us, and our portion from Numbers reveals great illustrations of New Testament truth.

God's channels of blessing are the noble ditchdiggers! These men had sense enough to know that if Israel was to receive the blessing of water from God (that 600,000 men beside women, children, and cattle might drink), someone should commence digging. God had the water supply, but ditches were needed to contain it.

It is noteworthy to see the titles given by God to the ditchdiggers: "princes and nobles." Years before they were slaves in Egyptian bondage. What a change! Now they were the nobility of God and not ashamed to dig ditches either. Bringing this to our present application, God needs ditchdiggers today and from the midst of His redeemed children. Are you one? The inference is obvious, for without any labor on our part, God cannot bless His people in this way.

Literal ditchdigging is considered one of the lowliest professions of earth and backbreaking; but applying it spiritually, it is a most profitable enterprise for Christian character! Why? Because it removes a lot of earth, providing God with a channel He can fill. There is too much of earth in most of us and removing it from our lives and from our assemblies would bring about the means of blessing. I heard of a prizefighter who, in order to keep himself in top-notch condition, took every ditchdigging job he could, claiming he could dig a hole fourteen feet deep and still throw the earth out. Oh, for the spiritual counterpart! The man would certainly be out of sight, but the blessings of God would have a deep channel to flow through, for God can fill any sized ditch we can dig!

There is not only the removal of the earth involved, but following this will be the supplying of the water, the needed blessings. This brings us to that which the Spirit of God ministers for blessing, the Word of God. It implies more digging, so to speak, but this time into the Holy Scriptures. "Study [or be diligent] to show thyself approved unto God, a workman that needeth not to be ashamed, rightly dividing the word of truth" (2 Tim. 2:15). Who are God's noble ditchdiggers today but those who empty themselves of earthly hindrances for the obvious purpose of filling themselves with the Word of God. They dig into the Scriptures, ever mindful that "All Scripture is given by inspiration of God, and is profitable for doctrine, for reproof, for correction, for instruction in righteousness; that the man of God may be perfect [or complete], throughly furnished unto all good works" (2 Tim. 3:16-17).

Note also that the nobles digged "under the direction of the lawgiver" who was, in their case we presume, Moses their leader. How blessed is the truth that Christ is the Head of the Church, His Body, and all the members are to be subservient to His authority! Would that this were more manifested today! For no flow of the Spirit's power and blessing can be apart from this relationship of Christ to His beloved people below.

The princes and nobles used "their staves"—fitting type of the Word of God which is the believer's only weapon and tool. It is indeed the sword of the Spirit, appointed for all phases of spiritual work in connection with the testimony today. Then with a Risen Head above, the Holy Spirit on earth and the Word of God in our hands, where are the ditchdiggers? Those who in their own lives and in connection with assembly responsibility, will prove that God still is able through the energy of faith to give "rivers of living waters." May God help you and me to be one of His noble ditchdiggers, for His name's sake.

"Then Israel sang this song, Spring up, O well; sing ye unto it." God's command and promise produced a response from Israel as they thus sang. It is significant that their words, "Sing ye unto it," can be literally translated "answer or respond to it!" The command and promise of God's Word today can only be carried through to completion in the energy of faith that is found in exercised hearts. The saints today should manifest this energy toward the ministry of the Holy Spirit, which the springing well typifies.

Jesus said in John 4:14, "Whosoever drinketh of the water that I shall give him shall never thirst; but the water that I shall give him shall be in him a well of water springing up into everlasting life." He is the Giver and His gift is the Holy Spirit, through Whose ministry the blessings of God for His people today come, flowing down from their Risen Head in heaven. The Spirit of God and His ministry is the springing well for us today!

What is faith's response? Is it some blind and unintelligent attitude toward His person and work, which is sometimes apparent among some professing spiritual movements? Certainly not! Faith is not blind. "Faith is the substantiating [or assurance, or firm conviction] of things hoped for, the conviction of things not seen" (Heb. 11:1, JND Trans.). It is the confidence that manifests we believe God will do as He declares in His Word. Yet there is to be an intelligent apprehension as to how He will do it. This fact is revealed in Romans 12:1-2, "I beseech you therefore, brethren, by the compassions of God, to present your bodies a living sacrifice, holy, acceptable to God, which is your intelligent service. And be not conformed to this world, but be ye transformed by the renewing of your mind, that ye may prove what is the good and acceptable and perfect will of God" (JND Trans.). It is not only a heart desire but also a rational apprehension of God's will and never anything irrational, based wholly upon the revealed Word of God.

This necessitates a true knowledge of how the Spirit of God works in this present age, for there is a great loss if we do not know the special ways in which it is the will of God to have the Spirit honored. The understanding of it should be in a twofold direction. First; as an individual saint, I should know the Spirit's work for my personal testimony. The New Testament reveals Him to be the One who indwells, seals, leads, fills, restrains, and teaches, among other things, so that as I study the Scriptures concerning Him, my yieldedness to the will of God is sensibly based on a clear knowledge of the Spirit's work in me, for me, and through me. Second; there is the corporate testimony to which I belong, the local assembly, over which the sovereign rights and actions of the Holy Spirit are to be known. New Testament teaching of church conduct and character is still the work of the Holy Spirit as in apostolic days, revealing the responsibility of the saints toward the corporate testimony of our Lord on earth.

Without the affectionate and intelligent yieldedness of the believers, the Spirit cannot effectively minister as He wants to. We must not be disobedient to His claims and the manner in which the Word of God declares He must work. What, then, is the response to faith? Is it not that exercised hearts will diligently search the Scriptures concerning the doctrine and work of the Holy Spirit, for an intelligent knowledge of the "springing well" and then bow in complete submission to His authority as the Word of God's chief Agent? This will again cause us to repeat the song of Israel, "Spring up, O well," and the "rivers of living water" will flow.

8
By Faith: Enoch's Homecoming

The world today does not realize that its ungodliness is about to be visited with divine judgment. As it was before the flood, men today are far from being convinced that judgment is near. Of men in Noah's day, Jesus said, They knew not until the flood came, and took them all away" (Mt. 24:39). Why did they not know? Had not Noah preached 120 years before the flood? (Gen. 6:3). They definitely heard his message but did not believe it. Therefore, they did not know until it happened! Then they knew, but it was too late. So will it be for those who today reject the message of salvation and refuse to flee from coming judgment. Yet it is our responsibility to endeavor to snatch them out of the fire (Jude 23).

Enoch was a man who stood for God against the times. And at the end of his life he was vindicated by God. "By faith Enoch was translated that he should not see death" (Heb. 11:5). Why was this attributed to Enoch as an act of faith? Did his faith spread her wings and bear the patriarch out of this scene and from the natural death he expected? If faith could do this, many a saint would attempt to fly away and be at rest (see Ps. 55:6). Yet faith in itself can accomplish no such thing. This power belongs to God alone, and so it is written of Enoch that "God took him" (Gen. 5:23), and he "was not found because God had translated him" (Heb. 11:5).

But it is the realm of faith to believe God. As He had revealed to Enoch that He was pleased with his testimony, and that judgment was coming on the world, so God also gave him the honor that he should not taste death but be translated without dying. Enoch believed it and lived in the power of its expectation, patiently awaiting that wonderful moment. So it is written, "By faith he was translated." In this way it is accredited to Enoch as an act of faith. Faith does not believe what it wants to believe and have it come to pass! The true basis of all faith is God and His Word.

God's Word records four prominent features in the life of Enoch that should be true of all who comprise the Church. First, Enoch walked with God (Gen. 5:22). Second, he had the testimony that he pleased God (Heb. 11:5). Third, he prophesied concerning the ungodly (Jude 14-15). Fourth, by faith he was translated (Heb. 11:5).

1. *Enoch walked with God.* The other patriarchs listed in Genesis 5 are declared to have "lived" and "died"—nothing more! Of Enoch it is added: "he walked with God," and that "he was not for God took him" (Gen. 5:22). The difference of character in these men of early history can be instructive to us (Rom. 15:4; 1 Cor. 10:11). They were all men in the line of Seth, yet of most of them it is said that he "lived" so long and then he "died." Enoch is the only one of whom it is written that he walked with God and then did not see death.

What dignity and honor was conferred on Enoch in the midst of the moral ruin before the Flood—to "walk with God." Is it possible that men of God may live and die upon the earth and not enjoy the privilege of walking with God? We must not be content to live without this experience today; we also should "walk with God." Yet to walk with God we must be in agreement with Him, for how "can two walk together except they be agreed?" (Amos 3:3). Without this, it is impossible; to do this we must be in harmony with God, giving up our own will and ways. It is unreasonable for us to expect God to give up His. Nor could we desire this. Enoch must have yielded his will to God, doing so "by faith," for it is impossible to please Him without "faith" (Heb. 11:6). He walked with God 300 years while in the midst of a wicked world, and while experiencing all the cares and trials of family life. He did not permit these conditions to hinder his walk with God. May we also seek to do the same.

2. *Enoch had the testimony that he pleased God.* This was the result of his walk with God, for God will never withhold this testimony from those who walk with Him. It is not a testimony of *acceptance* such as Abel had—in common with all who are accepted through the excellent sacrifice of Christ (Heb. 11:4). This testimony that Enoch obtained was because of his walk. If we desire the same, it is dependent upon ourselves and our walk as well.

Paul desired and labored for this, not being satisfied without it: "Wherefore also are we zealous, whether present or absent, to be agreeable to [or accepted with] Him" (2 Cor. 5:9). This testimony our Lord Jesus Christ desired us to possess and value. (See John 14:21.) The manifestation of Himself to our hearts is made contingent on our obedience to His Word and love to His Person. To have the abiding presence of both the Father and the Son manifested to us, will bring the testimony that we please God and walk with Him by faith, also contingent on our love for His Person and our obedience to His Word. (See John 14:23.) In this way we shall please God.

3. *Enoch prophesied concerning the ungodly.* Enoch faithfully gave testimony to the ungodly world through which he passed, warning it of God's displeasure of its sinful character. He also proclaimed coming judgment: "Behold, the Lord cometh with ten thousands of His saints, to execute judgment upon all, and to convince all that are ungodly among them of all their ungodly deeds which they have ungodly committed, and of all their hard speeches which ungodly sinners have spoken against him" (Jude 14-15). This testimony had been received from God and, being convinced of its divine certainty, he vigorously proclaimed the coming judgment.

We have abundance of Scripture to support such a testimony today, but are we faithfully declaring to this world the message of divine judgment which is now imminent? The message of Enoch was partly fulfilled in Noah's day, but is stated in such terms that indicate a future judgment when the Lord comes. This subject is part of the Church's testimony to the world in this present day. Are we faithfully declaring it?

4. *By faith he was translated.* Beloved, we today have a word of

similar character for our faith to rest upon; a divine promise of a blessed translation out of this world (1 Thess. 4:15-17). Do we believe it? Are we living in the power of it and patiently awaiting it? Are we enduring all things in life by the immediate prospect of this event? Shall we really be expecting Him when He comes?

Many saints have died in the faith of this promise and surely their faith will be accredited to them. But Enoch's act of faith is available to all those who are alive and remain when Jesus comes. When that wonderful event takes place, all living saints will be "caught up" with the resurrected ones. But of how many of the living saints will it be said, "By faith he (or she) was translated!" If our Lord came for us today, how many would say, "Lord, I knew it! You promised to come for me and I was waiting for You!" (See 1 Thess. 1:10). Would it not be wonderful to be looking for Him the moment He comes? Should we not like this to be said of us? May our heart answer before the Lord, for if there is affection enough to desire it, He is able to make it true of us for His glory and our blessing.

Wouldn't it be wonderful if Jesus came today?
Wouldn't it be wonderful if we were caught away?
To be with Him forevermore and ne'er from Him to stray—
Wouldn't it be wonderful if Jesus came today?

Until that blessed moment arrives, we should earnestly seek to exhibit the four prominent features that were found in the life of the patriarch Enoch: let us walk with God; let us please God; let us prophesy for God; and let us, by faith, be translated to God.

9
Saints in Wrong Places

God's Word records glaring examples of saints who tragically stepped out of fellowship with God, forfeiting their place of joy and blessing. These defections "are written for our admonition" we are told in 1 Corinthians 10:11. Consider some:

1. *Abraham in Egypt:* "And Abraham went down into Egypt" (Gen. 12:10). From "a mountain—an altar—a pilgrim tent" (Gen. 12:8), failing to trust God in time of famine, he departed on a downward path toward Egypt. His spiritual decline is evidenced by his conduct that followed.

Having forsaken the path of obedience, he resorted to the use of half truths in order to save his life from Pharaoh, all because of his attractive wife, Sarah. It was a shameful act for a saint of God, for "a lie that is half a truth is the blackest of lies." Yet in mercy and grace, God delivered him and restored him to his previous place of fellowship (Gen. 13:3). Back to Bethel, "the house of God," he arrived. He was again in his right place, but the results of his defection remain today.

From Egypt, he brought the Egyptian maid Hagar with him, who later became the mother of Ishmael by Abraham. Ishmael is the reputed progenitor of the burgeoning world of Islam, computed to be over 200 million. Next to Christianity, the Islamic religion is the most aggressive force, fanatically antagonistic to both Judaism and Christianity. All this is the result of one brief visit to Egypt!

Also, the sin of one man can be easily repeated, for in Genesis 20:2, Abraham again practiced the same shameful subterfuge in

Gerar. Years later, his son Isaac did the same (Gen. 26:7). What hatred and strife still prevails between the descendants of Ishmael and Isaac in the Middle East. What a solemn lesson all this is for us to consider; what happens when a saint gets into the wrong place and with what tragic, lasting results.

2. *Lot in Sodom:* Many may ask, "Was Lot a saint?" Let God's Word answer in 2 Peter 2:7-8, where he is described as "just Lot...that righteous man...his righteous soul." What is his story? Undoubtedly Abraham had been a spiritual influence on him until the time of their separation (Gen. 13). It was then that the defection of Lot's heart was revealed, not suddenly, but in a gradual process.

First, the lust of his eyes directed his interest toward Sodom (Gen. 13:10). Second, he "pitched his tent toward Sodom" (Gen. 13:12). Third, he settled right inside Sodom and became a leading figure of some importance. But truly he was a saint in the wrong place. Fourth, he even addressed his immoral companions in Sodom as "brethren" (Gen. 19:1, 6-7). It may have been his well-meaning intention to better the citizens of Sodom, but no saint in a wrong place can expect to make the world better.

Mercifully, God delivered Lot and his daughters from Sodom before its destruction. Yet, in spite of the divine deliverance, he further disgraced himself as a child of God, becoming the father of Ammon and Moab by his own two daughters. This moral disaster was far worse than even the loss of his wife and his possessions. He is a tragic example of a saved soul with a wasted life.

He has long since departed this scene, yet his defection and its results continue to spread. The descendants of Ammon and Moab are still among the irreconcilable and bitterest enemies of God's earthly people Israel today. Their hatred has been perpetual and will continue to the end of the age, until the Messiah of Israel returns, when all His foes will be subjugated under His reign (Ps. 2:8-9; 72:9). What repercussions can result when a saint gets into the wrong place! How careful we should be, for how many saints have we today who are in the wrong place? Are we careful ourselves to stay in obedience to the Word of God and in fellowship with Him?

An obvious lesson for us is this: a child of God cannot sin

without suffering. If we desire to disobey God, then we should seek to find a place where He cannot see us! Let the words of Psalm 139:23-24 be our earnest prayer.

3. *Miriam outside the camp* (Num. 12): Alas! is it possible that one of the leading saints among the women of Israel is found in the wrong place? Miriam, "the prophetess" who led the song of triumph on the shores of the Red Sea! The fragrant ointment of her testimony was spoiled by a "dead fly" getting in (Eccl. 10:1). With Aaron her brother, she spoke "against Moses because of the Ethiopian woman he had married" (Num. 12:1). What had his marriage to do with God speaking through him? Ostensibly, the accusation was against his marriage, but in reality it was aimed at his unique position before God. Why rake up the past after forty years? Yet the green-eyed monster of jealousy had been as a burning flame for a long time before their evil speaking!

God miraculously intervened on behalf of His servant, smiting Miriam immediately with leprosy and imposing temporary excommunication outside the camp, with a stern rebuke to Aaron the brother. For seven days, the nation of Israel made no progress until the punishment was past; they could not move. What a lesson for us today, to realize that corporate testimonies can be hindered from making spiritual progress because of the use of an unbridled tongue. The words of James 3 in regard to evil speaking are advisable to prayerfully read. Evil speaking is like a stone thrown up in the air; it comes down on the head of the person who threw it!

4. *The Israelites in the wilderness* (read Num. 13 & 14): A whole congregation of two to three million wandered in the wilderness an additional thirty-eight years because of unbelief and a refusal to obey God's command to enter Canaan. Two years after leaving Egypt, they were only a few days from the promised land. The sending of spies by the people (not by God) to bring a report back regarding the land ended in a great spiritual tragedy. Ten spies reported nothing but strong walled cities and giants in the land too great to conquer. They had a very little God. Two others, Joshua and Caleb, knew they had a big God and that, by comparison, the giants were very small. The

result—God's judgment hastily fell, destroying the ten spies of evil report and ordering the whole nation to turn back into the wilderness to wander until that generation had perished.

What an example for the Church to profit by. God has even found it needful to remove churches of His people through this age. Where are the seven churches of Asia today? (Rev. 2 and 3). They have long since disappeared and this has been the repeated history through the centuries, even in our present generation. "Take heed, brethren, lest there be in any of you an evil heart of unbelief, in departing from the living God" (Heb. 3:12).

5. *Samson in the prison house* (Jud. 16): Here was Samson in the wrong place: "And he did grind in the prison house" (Jud. 16:21). He was once the terror of the Philistines, but now shorn of his strength, he became the object of their sport. He had been divinely ordained to be Israel's great deliverer from their enemies, but now the Philistines were gathered in religious convocation to honor their idol-god Dagon and to celebrate the downfall of Samson. Poor blind Samson! What a pitiful character at the end of his life, in spite of the victory in death which God permitted. From his Nazarite vow he had fallen, step by step, gradually and consistently yielding to the passions and the lusts of the flesh. What a spiritual tragedy!

Has not this been repeated in the history of saints in our age, when those who have once been used greatly by God, instead of walking in the Spirit, have yielded to fleshly lusts, losing their power with God and their testimony with men? Is it not even today being known? The lesson of Lot being in Sodom warns us to beware of the world. The lesson of Samson warns us to beware of the flesh. Samson, a man of abnormal physical strength by divine endowment, revealed himself to be one of amazing moral weakness. Yes, he was a saint, one of God's chosen servants, but at the end of his life, he was in the wrong place.

Where are we today? All saints are heaven-born and heaven-bound: But all are not heaven-bent! What about you and what about me? These things were written aforetime for our learning (1 Cor. 10:11).

6. *David on the roof* (2 Sam. 11:1-5): The wrong place can some-

times be close to the right place with a short, easy path between. How sad it is to read of an eminent and experienced saint, as King David on the roof of the royal palace in the wrong place! It was the time of the year when kings went forth to battle and David was urgently needed on the battlefield, not at home. The national peace and security of Israel was frequently in danger from their enemies who were anxious to settle old scores; yet at such a time we read that "David tarried still at Jerusalem" (2 Sam. 11:1). The reason for doing so is not revealed, but the tragic result is written for our learning. Rising from bed in a state of restlessness, David wandered aimlessly to the rooftop and saw what he ought not to have seen because he was in the wrong place.

After his initial sin with Bathsheba, the sin of murder followed in the death of Uriah the Hittite, her husband. When one seeks to cover up sin, it is often followed by another. The conduct of David is inexplicable, practicing such guile to hide his guilt. But God is holy and righteous—and loved David too deeply to allow him to be unchallenged, unopposed, and unpunished (Heb. 12:6). Though in mercy God forgave him when he sobbed out his soul in repentance and penitential grief (Ps. 51), yet the scars of divine discipline remained for years. His sin was not the indiscretion of a thoughtless youth but the transgression of mature manhood. Advanced years offer no protection from sinning. What a solemn lesson this is for us, to beware of the lust of the eyes and the flesh, by keeping ourselves in the right place! When we are where we ought not to be we see things we ought not to see. May God's grace keep us in the right place.

7. *Jehoshaphat and Ahab* (2 Chron. 18): Jehoshaphat joined affinity with wicked King Ahab of Israel and during the entire period proved himself to be in the wrong place. He made the first overture in the ungodly alliance by visiting Ahab. In so honoring Ahab by his presence, he then was snared into making a promise to join forces with him in battle. "I am as thou art and my people are thy people" (1 Ki. 22:4). In the battle that followed at Ramoth-Gilead, but for God's grace and protective power, King Jehoshaphat would have been slain. However, it

was King Ahab who was slain in the purpose of God, and Jehoshaphat was allowed to return to Jerusalem in peace (2 Chron. 19:1).

Through God's servant, the prophet, Jehoshaphat was sternly rebuked, "Shouldest thou help the ungodly and love them that hate the Lord? (2 Chron. 19:2). Yet the king failed to learn his lesson and later formed an alliance with Ahab's son (2 Ki. 3:6-7).

How slow the saints can be to learn from our lessons of divine discipline today. We must realize that it is an evil thing when God's people form unhallowed, compromising associations with the sinners of the world. God's Word is plain about this problem and specifically forbids an unequal yoke (read 2 Cor. 6:14-16). Righteousness is opposed to unrighteousness; light is opposite to darkness; Christ is against Belial; believers are different from infidels; and the temple of God is contrary to all idols.

The unequal yoke of believers with unbelievers under any circumstances is dishonoring and displeasing to God, whether it be religious, commercial, or matrimonial. It can prove to be disastrous to the saint and his testimony if thus ensared. God may mercifully intervene and deliver, but His plain commands should not be minimized, for when they are; His disciplinary measures will surely follow. We should never compromise with the ungodly world for to do so will lead the saint into the wrong place.

Ponder the truth of the following words: God gave His Son to the world, and the world sent Him back to the Father with the marks of their causeless hatred upon His body! Shall I make friendships with it?

To compromise with the world is to forget and disregard the words of the Lord Jesus, "If the world hate you, ye know that it hated Me before it hated you. If ye were of the world, the world would love his own; but because ye are not of the world, therefore the world hateth you" (Jn. 15:18-19). Is He right?

10
Elijah's Last Journey

On his last mission (2 Ki. 2:1-14), Elijah visited places in Israel that were famous in spiritual history. Mighty evidences of God's presence and His power were associated with each.

1. *Gilgal:* "Elijah went with Elisha from Gilgal" (2 Ki. 2:1). Gilgal was the first place of encampment after Israel crossed Jordan (Josh. 4:19-20). It became the place of circumcision—the cutting off of the flesh (Josh. 5:2-8). It was also where the final reproach of Egypt was rolled away (Josh. 5:9). The first passover was commemorated there as well (Josh. 5:10-11). It became the base of Israel's military operations as they conquered the Promised Land.

The past glories of Gilgal must have flooded the prophet's mind as he left the city behind. Gilgal was now a place with no divine power. The flesh prevailed over the people and the testimony of God. The reproach of Egypt had returned upon Israel and spiritual victories were turned to spiritual defeats. All this Elijah felt in his sensitive soul as he left Gilgal. Is this not parallel to the professing Church today?

2. *Bethel:* "The Lord hath sent me to Bethel" (2 Ki. 2:2). Jacob named Bethel long ago (Gen. 28:10-22). He revealed three abiding principles associated with Bethel.

a) It was "none other than the house of God," His dwelling place on the earth.

b) It had a ladder of communication by which God's people could climb to heights of heavenly glory, for it was the "gate of heaven."

c) God's grace and faithfulness to His people was assured them (Gen. 28:13-15). Elijah valued these principles in his heart and life.

However, Bethel became a place of idolatry, where Jeroboam's golden calf was the object of worship. It kept the ten tribes from going to God's house in Jerusalem (1 Ki. 12:28-33). The king was not interested in climbing to heights of heavenly glory and leading God's people heavenward. In accordance with the passions of his own heart, strengthened by the idolatrous system he set up, he led Israel in paths of selfishness, greed, and earthly gain. The meaning of Bethel, "the house of God," became unknown in experience. The soul of Elijah tasted the bitterness of this fact.

This also is analogous with the present condition of the processing Church today. "The house of God" is in great disorder, signally failing in "the last days" to prove itself to be God's habitation on earth. (Compare 1 Tim. 3:15 with 2 Tim. 2:20-21.) It is not "the gate of heaven" where spiritual blessings are known in power, for earthly things have become more important than heavenly things. Instead of proving God's grace and faithfulness to maintain the testimony, the independence of the flesh prevails.

3. *Jericho:* "The Lord hath sent me to Jericho" (2 Ki. 2:4). Israel's first and greatest victory was won here (Josh. 6). The idolatrous and wicked city was destroyed and God's curse placed upon the rebuilding of it (Josh. 6:26). What were the thoughts of Elijah as he came to Jericho? During Ahab's wicked reign, "did Hiel the Bethelite build Jericho" (1 Ki. 16:34). He defied and also bore God's curse as he rebelled against the Word of God, though men called it "the city of palm trees."

Is there not a parallel in the professing Church today? Are not the walls of Jericho built again? Is not the character of the Satanic world system deeply imprinted upon the present outward testimony? Where are the victories of faith and how many walls are being broken down today by spiritual conquest?

4. *Jordan:* "The Lord hath sent me to Jordan" (2 Ki. 2:6). What divine power had been associated with Jordan. As a great nation, Israel crossed over Jordan on dry ground, though the

mighty river "flowed over all his banks" (Josh. 4:18). In resurrection power, the Lord brought them across with the sacred Ark of God, the symbol of His presence, in the midst of the river. Twelve stones were erected for an eternal memorial in the river bed; and twelve stones erected as a testimony to God's power on the shores of Canaan. Figuratively, they came through death in the power of resurrection.

As Elijah smote the waters to pass over, Jordan and its memorials had no significance to Israel. This he knew, for the God of resurrection power was now unknown in the nation. The past glories were now darkened in the mind of the prophet because of the present weakness of Israel. It would seem that Elijah and Elisha were only left to prove the God of resurrection power as they crossed over Jordan.

And today? Where is the resurrection power of God known in the professing Church? How little we know of it in our individual lives as believers (Phil. 3:10).

5. *The Wilderness:* In the past, Israel made great progress in traveling from the wilderness into Canaan, encamping at Gilgal, going forward to conquer Jericho, and ultimately building "the house of God." Now Elijah has retraced their historic path backward, arriving from whence Israel came—the wilderness. What did it mean to the prophet? His mind had undoubtedly been filled with memories of God's glory and power that once was known among His people, but now none of these places had any attraction for his heart; they all had failed. The present crisis had become a moral and spiritual wilderness to God's servant. He had but one hope and one goal. His Master had promised to take him to Heaven!

6. *From the Wilderness to Heaven:* "And Elijah went up by a whirlwind into heaven" (2 Ki. 2:11). Gilgal, Bethel, Jericho, Jordan, and the wilderness left behind! All the existing conditions in Israel left, too. The great *political* crisis caused by Ahab's ungodly reign would meet its predicted doom and Ahab himself would be slain (2 Chron. 18). The great *ecclesiastical* power behind the throne, Queen Jezebel, would end in a gruesome death as predicted (2 Ki. 9:30-37). The whole situation had produced nothing but a moral and a spiritual wilderness for God's

servant the prophet; yet what a happy man! God had revealed to him a better way of departure from life than death—his rapture to heaven! Farewell Ahab and Jezebel! The apostasy would be left to its final doom. Farewell to failing Gilgal, Jericho, Bethel, Jordan, and also the barren wilderness! The glories of heaven were now before him. The face of His Master he soon would see. What happiness must have flooded his heart. The last destination of his journey—Heaven!

Beloved, does not this parallel our situation today? The whole political and ecclesiastical scene under Satan's rule is fast creating a moral and spiritual wilderness for the people of God. Yet how blessed is our hope. Oh! happy people! We also have but one hope and one goal:

"For this we say unto you by the Word of the Lord, that we which are alive and remain unto the coming of the Lord shall not [precede] them which are asleep. For the Lord Himself shall descend from heaven with a shout, with the voice of the archangel, and with the trump of God; and the dead in Christ shall rise first: then we which are alive and remain shall be caught up together with them in the clouds, to meet the Lord in the air: and so shall we ever be with the Lord. Wherefore comfort one another with these words" (1 Thess. 4:15-18).

11
The Blessings of Old Age

This subject may not appeal to some folks, but for those who have reached the sunset days of life, a study of it will prove helpful and encouraging. For others, let me suggest that you try to enter into its message or save it until you find yourself in the classification of old age!

There can be nothing more beautiful than the declining days of a believer in the Lord Jesus. The character of an aged believer should be more attractive than ever, and though the light of this earthly life may be fading and the shadows deepening, there should be an increasing mellowness, sweetness, and serenity of spirit. "We all do fade as a leaf," writes Isaiah (Isa. 64:6). "Yet the leaf is never so beautiful as when it is faded. No artist ever painted a picture so beautiful as the panorama of woodlands transfigured with indescribable mingling of gold, crimson, and saffron, as if a flood of divine glory swept across them."

First, consider the joy of possessing Christ as your Saviour in old age. There was an old man named Simeon. God revealed to him that he would not die before he had seen the Lord's Christ (read Lk. 2:25-35). The Spirit of God led him into the temple as Joseph and Mary entered with "the child Jesus, to do for him after the custom of the law. Then took he Him up in his arms, and blessed God, and said, Lord, now lettest Thou Thy servant depart in peace, according to Thy word, for mine eyes have seen Thy salvation."

The blessed Saviour was embraced in his arms! How precious at the end of his life was such a blessing. Have you embraced

Him? Is your heart and soul wrapped around the Saviour? Simeon had no eyes for Joseph and Mary at that moment. Just for "the child Jesus." This One was God's salvation. No matter how dear are loved ones of earth at the end of life, the Saviour transcends them all. It makes the departure from earth one of peace for Simeon. No wonder he "blessed God." What a wonderful end to a long life—arms around the Saviour and eyes upon Him, his lips also praising God! May this be your end and mine.

Second, consider the joy of speaking of Christ in old age. At the end of life, if we have known Him, the testimony should be much greater and clearer, than that of a young believer. Linked with the incident of Simeon is the adoration of an old woman named Anna, recorded in Luke 2:36-38. She was a prophetess of great age, widowed after seven years of marriage. At the time of the temple incident, she had been a widow for eighty-four years, and would be well over one hundred years of age. She had served God night and day through those years, with fastings and prayers. A descendant of the tribe of Asher (meaning *happy*), she probably was a happy child of God, but her joy was made greater when she also saw "the child Jesus."

Immediately her lips broke forth with praise Godward: "She...gave thanks likewise unto the Lord." Hallelujah! must have been the word in her heart and mouth! Then, knowing that "the joy of the Lord is your strength" (Neh. 8:10), she set forth to visit all the saints in Jerusalem: she "spake of Him to all them that looked for redemption." Praise Godward and testimony manward! The usual infirmity of old age meant nothing in the joy of seeing Him. It certainly takes Christ to make old people happy at the end of life and He is able!

Now consider the joy of leaving earth and going to be "with the Lord." If saved, Christ is your own and you are His own. The Word declares, "Blessed (happy) are the dead who die in the Lord" (Rev. 14:13). "Happy to die?" you ask. Why not? Listen to the words of the saintly M'Cheyne:

"The world says, 'Blessed are the living,' but God says, 'Blessed are the dead'! The world judges things by reason and sense, as they appear outwardly to men. God judges things by what they really are. He looks at things in their real color and magnitude. The world says, 'Better is a living dog than a dead lion.' The world looks on their families in the fresh bloom of health, with bounding step and elasticity of youth, possessed with luxuries and long, bright summer days ahead, and the world says, 'There is a happy soul.' But God takes us into the dark shadows where a child of His lies cold in death. He points to the pale face where death sits enthroned, the cheeks wasted by long disease, the eye glazed in death, the stiff hands folded over the bosom, the loved ones and friends weeping around— and He whispers in our ears, 'Blessed are the dead'!"

If it is happy to have His smile here, how much happier to have His smile there! If it is sweet to have an anchor within "the veil," how much better to be there, where no gloom can come. If it be joyful to walk with Him here, how much more joyous to be with Him there. For in His presence "is fullness of joy"; at His right hand "there are pleasures forevermore" (Ps. 16:11).

But be careful! This is not true of all the dead. Only a minority are so blest, according to the testimony of Jesus: "Few there be that find it"(see Mt. 7:13-14). There is no blessing for the Christless dead: they rush into eternity where God writes not "Blessed" but "Cursed" for "He that believeth shall be saved: he that believeth not shall be damned."

Consider what it means to be "in the Lord." Everyone who is blessed in dying has been saved. They were "born again." They were awakened to see themselves lost, undone, hopeless, and in need of the Saviour. The Lord Jesus drew near and revealed Himself. They believed on Him as the One who died for all their sins. They believed and were happy. That was their beginning of being "in the Lord." So when death comes, their happiness does not disappear, nor decrease. Rather, it becomes greater. Praise the Lord!

There is no evil where the dead in the Lord are: no pain; no toil; no heartaches; no sorrows; no burdens; no struggles! "They rest from their labors." Oh, how blest they are that die "in the Lord." If you are an aged believer, lay hold of these facts. If younger, store them up in your heart for time ahead! "The Blessings of Old Age" are a reality and many other contributory facts from God's Word could be added. Let us not consider old age as going "downhill," as some suggest. It is not so! Not for a believer, as one has poetically suggested:

"But oh! it is not going down; 'tis climbing higher, higher!
Until we almost see the mansions that our souls desire;
For if the natural eye grows dim, it is but dim to earth,
While the eye of faith grows keener, to perceive the Saviour's worth.

"And when the eyes, now dim, shall open to behold the King,
And ears, now dull with age, shall hear the harps of heaven ring;
And on the head, now hoary, shall be placed the crown of gold,
Then shall be known the lasting joy of never growing old!"

12
God in the Stillness

"Be still, and know that I am God" (Psalm 46:10).

The prophetic words of the psalmist will soon be heard by all nations of people in the midst of worldwide convulsions of strife, hatred, bloodshed, and war. The powers of evil, energized by "the dragon, beast and false prophet" (see Rev. 13), will manifest the final rebellion of this age against the Lord and His anointed. Then the mighty God of glory, in the power of His majesty, will appear from heaven (Rev. 1:7; Rev. 19:11-21). It will be the inevitable judgment of this godless world (Jude 14-15). Then above the carnage and strife of men will be heard the voice of God's King, commanding all the earth: "Be still, and know that I am God! I will be exalted above the nations, I will be exalted in the earth."

The results will be conclusive. "The [nations] raged, the kingdoms were moved: He uttered His voice, the earth melted" (Ps. 46:6). It will be a day of complete defeat for Satan and the nations, one of total victory for the godly remnant of Israel, the Church, and the saved out of the nations. The glorious reign of Christ will commence; His chosen people shall be gathered around their King. The throne of His worldwide dominion will be established, all nations bowing at His feet. May this day soon come!

Let us turn from this prophetic view, however, and learn some practical lessons for our daily path. The peaceful reign of quietness should speak to our hearts of present truth that can be enjoyed by us while in this world of perplexity and distress. The benevolent reign of the One who is God's King should already have begun in the hearts of His people.

GOD CAN BE KNOWN IN QUIETNESS

"Be still and *know* that I am God." Comparatively speaking, God is little known today in this materially-minded world. As one has soliloquized: "There was a time when the living God was a reality to men. Then He became merely an influence; now He is merely an opinion." Yet among the human race, God's children should be taking time to know Him in the quietness of His presence. A noted theologian has written, "To know this mighty Being, as far as He may be known, is the noblest aim of human necessity, that believers should resolutely refuse to permit the encroachment of other things to rob us of the time required for meditation, the study of God's Word, and prayer." Let us seek faithfully to "Be still" and "know God" (2 Pet. 3:18).

GOD'S DELIVERANCE IS FOUND IN QUIETNESS

The problems of life constantly appear in our path. Red Sea experiences, similar in character to Israel's, may show no visible escape for us. Pause to hear the words of Moses: "Fear ye not, stand still, and see the salvation of the Lord" (Ex. 14:13). In such circumstances, the obvious lesson of quietness is to learn that "the Lord shall fight for you, and ye shall hold your peace" (Ex. 14:14). To do nothing and to say nothing is a very different lesson. To "hold your peace" means to "keep quiet!" Plain talk, perhaps, but what we often need.

Take another lesson from the life of Jehoshaphat in 2 Chronicles 20. Read it through and see how, in quietness and prayer before the Lord, a great deliverance was accomplished without the use of one earthly instrument of warfare by God's people! There are occasions when the deliverance needed must come in this way—for God's glory and for our great joy.

STRENGTH AND CONFIDENCE ARE FOUND THERE

To Israel, God said, "In returning and rest shall ye be saved: in quietness and in confidence shall be your strength: and ye would not" (Isa. 30:15). Israel rejected this counsel and suffered tragic consequences. They depended on swift horses and Egyptian allies, but in vain. God said, "Their strength is to sit still" (Isa. 30:7), but they said, "No! for we will flee upon horses" (Isa. 30:16). Many times we may be disposed to display our own wisdom in grappling with our dangers, when our safety lies in waiting only on God. "They that wait upon the Lord shall renew their strength; they shall mount up with wings as eagles; they shall run, and not be weary; and they shall walk and not faint." The secret of tranquility is to "rest in the Lord," producing confidence and strength within our hearts. "My soul, wait thou only upon God: for my expectation is from Him" (Ps. 62:5).

GOD'S GUIDANCE IS LEARNED IN QUIETNESS

"The Lord is my shepherd...He leadeth me beside the still waters...He leadeth me in the paths of righteousness" (Ps. 23). How frequently we need guidance in life's intricate maze, but it should be found in the retreat to the "green pastures" of God's Word and in the quietness of the "still waters" of His presence, when He can speak directly to our souls. It is there we hear the Shepherd's voice and can be led by His Spirit aright. Let us determine to take time from the frantic pace of modern living to have the blessing of quietness before Him.

CHRIST THE LORD KNEW THIS BLESSING

A greater life of human activity cannot be found than our Lord's. Yet in the midst of it, He devoted time to be in the presence of God His Father. "He wakeneth morning by morning, He wakeneth Mine ear to hear as the learned," prophesied Isaiah of Him (Isa. 50:4). "In the morning, rising up a great while before day, He went out, and departed into a solitary place, and there prayed" (Mk. 1:35). If He sought this in His human pathway, how much more should we!

> *"Whenever the Master could, He stole away*
> *From the great throngs, to seek some quiet place,*
> *Where He could be alone, where He could pray,*
> *Where God could come to meet Him face to face.*

Strange strength is ever borne of solitude;
The heart today grows weary of its care
And overburdened. God, it would be good
To seek a mountainside and find Thee there!

Christ stole away at evening to the hills.
So should we go, the press of the day's work done,
To seek some quiet place when the last light spills
The radiant splendor of the setting sun,
And kneel to pray! How often we have lost
The way to solitude, and at such a cost!"

There were occasions when He spent all night in prayer, as recorded in Luke 6:12, "He went out into a mountain to pray, and continued all night in prayer to God." The answer to the problem was known by daybreak, for "when it was day, He called unto Him His disciples" (v. 13).

May God the Holy Spirit enable us to learn the blessings of quietness, by daily practicing the enjoyment of His presence so that we shall have that inward peace and joy that alone can be maintained by a close fellowship with God. Let us hear Him say daily: "Be still and know that I am God."

13
The Valley of the Shadow

There are many valleys and canyons of human experience as we pass through life, each one possessing its darkness and dangers, whether mental, physical, or spiritual. Through them the believer proves the faithfulness of the Shepherd, who dispels the darkness, delivers from the danger, and lifts the heart above the despair into victory. Yet ultimately, the last valley is to be reached—the valley of the shadow of death! For some it may be difficult to face, and for others, not so difficult; but the "comfort of the Scriptures" can provide for the believer God's sustaining grace in such an hour. The Good Shepherd who has proved Himself to us in the valleys of life, will also prove Himself sufficient for this valley at the end of the journey. What He has been, He still will be: "that Great Shepherd of the Sheep" (Heb. 13:20). Let us heed the words of the sweet Psalmist of Israel as he expresses the deep conviction of his soul, and let us meditate confidently and joyfully on the precious truth he states in Psalm 23:4, "Yea, though I walk through the valley of the shadow of death, I will fear no evil; for Thou art with me." Note four precious facts that he reveals, which can be ours to comfort us in the valley of the shadow of death:

His Composure: The tranquility of his soul is indicated by the two words, "I walk." There was no evidence of terror or panic as he faced the last, dark valley; nothing but composure of mind. As he entered the vale, a deliberateness and steadiness of mind is seen, suggesting that he would pass calmly on his way through, permitting nothing and no one to cause alarm. With equanimity, he enters to walk with steady composure. He will not run in terror nor dart to and fro as if in panic. His progress will be calm, orderly, sedate. He will take the valley in his stride.

His Confidence: "I will walk *through,*" he declares. He is an in-transit passenger with a nonstop journey before him. He expresses no doubt as to the certainty of reaching the "desired haven." What blessed optimism and confidence he possessed. The valley may be dark; the mountains overshadowing on every side; the path rugged and steep, painful and sore. But the outcome was sure: "I will dwell in the house of the Lord forever." The end of the valley would bring him into eternal light out of the darkness; into eternal balm and out of pain; into eternal peace and forever free from the storms beneath. Instead of temporary pilgrimages on earth, he would then reach his eternal home with all its glory and bliss realized: "I will dwell in the house of the Lord forever." Home at last!

His Courage: "I will fear no evil" in this valley, states the psalmist. The former evils of life cannot touch me in this valley. We can name a few of these evils that are being left behind: *The evil of sin*, with its accompanying terror is left behind, for how can it press its claim any further? *The evil of self,* our many failures and shortcomings, are also terminating their power over us here. *The evil of Satan*, the great enemy of God and His people, who has harassed us through the days of our pilgrimage, will no longer be able to take advantage of us. *The evil of the world*, is fading forever from sight, and its vaunted riches, power, and glory possesses no attraction. It is vanishing away forever—"the world passeth away."

The evil tidings that can trouble the soul and darken the mind as we travel through this vale of tears, we shall leave them behind forever. *The evil conscience* which has tormented many unfortunate souls, shall then be cleared forever. How blessed to know this freedom. "How much more shall the blood of Christ...purge your conscience" (Heb. 9:14).

Upon his deathbed, an aged man said to me, "I'll be looking for your arrival in heaven."

"How do you know that you will be there?"

Replying, he triumphantly said, "I'm trusting the blood of

Jesus!" This is peace and triumph in the valley of death, enabling one to say, "I will fear no evil!"

His Companion: This last fact is the greatest and gives eternal value to all the preceding truths: "for Thou art with me." Blessed Companion—"The Lord is my Shepherd," and He who has traversed the valleys of life with me since I made Him mine, I can be assured will walk through the valley of death with me also.

My loved ones are unable to go with me: my friends cannot accompany me through this valley: I leave them all behind, but I cannot go through without Him! "That great Shepherd of the sheep" will be with me, escorting me through and bringing me into "the house of the Lord forever." It is worthy of note to discern that in the preceding verses of the psalm, David speaks about the Shepherd. Who else could be in the valley with him, but his Shepherd? He alone is the One to whom he can express his heart and rejoice that his Shepherd through life is the same Shepherd in death—with me!

It was the custom of a chaplain during World War I, when men were going to the front, to get them to repeat with him the opening clause of the Shepherd Psalm, marking it off on the fingers of their left hands. The little finger represented the word "The"; the next finger, "Lord"; the middle finger, "is"; the index finger, "my"; and the thumb, "Shepherd." He called it his Five Finger Exercise. every man was asked to mark the palm of his hand with indelible pencil to remind him of the text, and special stress was laid on the index finger—MY Shepherd—the finger that spoke of the personal appropriation of the shepherdly care.

After the battle of Bullecourt, one young fellow was found, quite dead, grasping firmly with his right hand the index finger of his left. The young soldier understood the secret. With an innumerable host of saints and heroes and martyrs, he rejoiced that he had a place peculiarly his own in the heart of the Good Shepherd, and clung to that sweet faith in perfect serenity to the last. So may you and I.

Two Scottish lassies on a bleak day in January 1681 were to be hung for worshipping God in a way forbidden by law. As they emerged from their cell, they were told to walk across the yard to the gallows. One said to the other, "Come on, Belle, this is our great day! Let us sing!" And she began:

> *The Lord's my Shepherd, I'll not want,*
> *He makes me down to lie*
> *In pastures green, He leadeth me*
> *The quiet waters by.*
>
> *Yea though I walk in death's dark vale,*
> *Yet I will fear no ill;*
> *For Thou art with me; and Thy rod*
> *And staff me comfort still.*

As they stood pinioned upon the fatal platform, they concluded their duet:

> *Goodness and mercy all my life*
> *Shall surely follow me;*
> *And in God's house for evermore*
> *My dwelling place shall be.*

Their composure, their confidence, and their courage was genuine because their Companion was the Lord Jesus Christ, the Good and Great Shepherd. May you and I enjoy the same, by His grace rejoicing in that precious truth: "The Lord is *my* Shepherd."

Part Two
The Blessed Hope

14
Crossroad of Eternity

One of the greatest crossroads of Christian experience is the last one in the normal course of events. The apostle Paul describes it when writing his own farewell to his beloved son in the faith, Timothy, "For I am now ready to be offered, and the time of my departure is at hand" (2 Tim. 4:6). His faithful devotion to his Master had brought him through many critical experiences safely, but now the final one was "at hand"—his departure into eternity. The word "departure" is of a special significance in the Greek text. The word *analuo* means "to unloose, or release; a metaphor that either is nautical, from loosing moorings preparatory to setting sail, or military, from breaking up an encampment."

For the apostle, it was launching into a new spiritual adventure, leaving the moorings of this life and setting sail toward the discoveries of eternal glories in another world far away from this present evil scene. He had previously expressed a longing to set out upon this journey to his beloved Philippian believers. He was torn between two desires: one to go and be with Christ, which was "far better"; and the other "to abide in the flesh" which seemed more necessary then for the saints (Phil. 1:23-24). However, now the moment was at hand and he joyfully writes, "the time of my release is come."

The occasion produced from his heart a concise and complete testimony of his Christian pilgrimage through the years past, together with a perfect assurance of what was before him as he set sail into eternity. His brief statement concerning it is stated in few words: "I have combated the good combat, I have finished the race, I have kept the faith. Henceforth the crown of righteousness is laid up for me, which the Lord, the righteous Judge, will render me in that day; but not only to me, but also to all who love His appearing" (2 Tim. 4:7-8, New Trans.). It was a satisfying retrospection of his life for Christ and a joyous anticipation of his future compensation, revealed to him right at the crossroad of eternity. Will it be ours? Meditate on his words:

The Retrospection of the Past (2 Tim. 4:7). His words reveal a life of victory through all his Christian testimony:

a) A Victorious Combat: "I have fought a good fight." The Christian warfare for all of us reveals a threefold enemy—the world, the flesh, and the devil. (See 1 Jn. 2:14-17; Rom. 7:18; Eph. 6:10-12.) The world could not conquer Paul, for he lived a life of victory over it (Gal. 6:14; Jn. 16:33). The inward enemy of the flesh, so powerful in us, Paul crucified and conquered it. What a victory! (Rom. 7:24-25; Gal. 2:20). The devil, the great enemy of God and man, mighty but not almighty, became a defeated foe before Paul through the use of God-given weapons for warfare (2 Cor. 10:3-5; Eph. 6:10-18). The battle raged daily but Paul was a victor. Are we?

> *"Fight the good fight with all thy might.*
> *Christ is thy strength, and Christ thy right;*
> *Lay hold on life, and it shall be*
> *Thy joy and crown eternally."*

b) A Victorious Race: "I have finished my race." He was about to cross the "tape line" at the end of his last stretch toward home and his Master who waited for him in glory. Others may have dropped out along the race, forfeiting their Christian testimony, but Paul ran right to the end of the allotted course. Will we? The secret of his victory is discovered in two facts. First, his spiritual condition—he kept himself in top form spiritually all the time. Physically, he often suffered weakness and infirmities, yet though the physical muscles and frame kept "perishing," daily his spiritual strength increased: "Though our outward man perish, yet the inward man is renewed day by day" (2 Cor. 4:16). Note his carefulness in this connection as stated in 1 Corinthians

9:24-27. Let us not be more concerned about our physical health than the spiritual shape.

Second, his spiritual objective—there is always a goal, a prize, at the end of the race, and Paul knew the great prize for him at the end of life was Christ in glory (Phil. 3:13-14). No one runs a race well if preoccupied with what is on the sidelines or what may be behind. We must keep our eyes on the goal at the end, which for us is the Lord Himself—to see Him! Then "let us run with patience the race that is set before us, looking unto Jesus, the author of faith" (Heb. 12:1-2).

> *"Run the straight race through God's good grace,*
> *Lift up thine eyes, and seek His face;*
> *Life with its way before us lies,*
> *Christ is the path, and Christ the prize."*

c) A Victorious Obedience: "I have kept the faith." We must not fail to realize the comprehensiveness of these five words. They reveal obedience to all the truth and the counsels of God as revealed in His Word. To the elders at Ephesus, Paul had said, "I have not shunned to declare unto you all the counsel of God" (Acts 20:27). And this statement is made by one who himself obeyed the truth that he preached to others. He sought all divine revelation in order to know what God required of him as an obedient servant, obeying the truth in each department of his life, publicly and privately. As the Lord said to Philadelphia, "Thou hast kept My Word," so He could give to Paul the same commendation. This was victorious obedience, something greatly lacking today in the corporate testimony of the Church. How many of us are concerned to know *all* the will of God for us and do it, taking corporate and individual responsibility?

> *"Faint not nor fear, His arm is near;*
> *He changeth not and thou art dear.*
> *Only believe, and thou shalt see,*
> *That Christ is all in all to thee."*

The Anticipation of the Future (2 Tim. 4:8). The one who lives a life of victory, as Paul did, will be confident of being acclaimed victor in eternity. Note this assurance:

a) **Paul's Confidence:** "Henceforth the crown of righteousness is laid up for me." The eternal reward would but confirm that he had been with God and had lived right for God. What a crown to covet! No greater honor can one receive "in that day" than to be publicly approved as to their testimony in life and that before all.

b) **Paul's Confessor:** It will be "the Lord, the righteous Judge" who will render the vindication and the apostle patiently and confidently waited for this to be done in the future day of glory. (See 1 Cor. 4:3-5 and 2 Tim. 1:12.)

c) **Paul's Concern:** "And not to me only but unto them also that love His appearing." His unselfish desire for others constrains him to encourage them to win the same triumph and glory as would be his. This is our opportunity; shall we seize it now?

> *"Cast care aside, lean on your Guide;*
> *His boundless mercy will provide.*
> *Trust, and your trusting soul shall prove,*
> *Christ is its life, and Christ its love."*

15
The Two Advents of Christ

"Out of him came forth the corner (cornerstone), out of him the nail, out of him the battle-bow, out of him every oppressor together [the absolute ruler]" (Zech. 10:4).

Here we have a glorious constellation of precious titles of Christ: the Cornerstone, the Nail, the Battle Bow, and the Absolute Ruler. They shine in brilliance and full of meaning to reveal the One who meets the need of our hearts while in this world. The first two titles definitely reveal the First Advent of our Saviour; the last two reveal the power and glory of His second Advent.

The Cornerstone: here is a Messianic title recorded in Isaiah 28:16 and applied by the Lord Himself in Matthew 21:42. Also it was used by the apostles in Acts 4:11 and 1 Peter 2:4-8. He is today the Foundation of His Church, for "we are built upon the foundation of the apostles and prophets" (Eph. 2:20-21). He is a "Sure Foundation" (Isa. 28:16; 2 Tim. 2:19). Upon Him the building is safe (Mt. 16:18). This is not only true corporately, but individually. Each believer can say, Christ is my Cornerstone.

The Nail: This Messianic title appears in Isaiah 22:21-25. Though addressed to Eliakim, it refers in its full meaning to the Messiah, the Christ. (Compare Rev. 3:7 with Isa. 22:22.) He is a *sure* Nail, fastened in a *sure* place, to bear burdens. He bore the burden of our sins (Isa. 53:6; 1 Pet. 2:24). He bears our cares and anxieties now (Ps. 55:22; 1 Pet. 5:7). Are we overwhelmed with trials? Let us cast them on Him and leave them there. We build our hopes for eternity on Him. We cast our cares and sorrows on Him. We should also give the glory of our lives all to Him. So let us enjoy the blessedness of saying, "Christ is my Nail."

The Battle Bow: Here is another title describing the character of Christ (Isa. 63; Ps. 110:5-6; Rev. 19:11), when, at His second coming He will have a sharp sword to smite the nations who have filled up to the brim their cup of iniquity. Then He will rule them with a rod of iron and dash them to pieces as a potter's vessel (Ps. 2:9). This is a solemn aspect of His character, but a necessary one to justify the holiness and justice of God.

He has been and will again be Israel's Battle Bow (Ex. 15:1-6; 2 Chron. 20:15; Isa. 37:36; Zech. 14:1-3). We ourselves have many battles to fight; against Satan, the world and self. Yet it is written, "We are more than conquerors through Him that [loveth] us" (Rom. 8:37). We have the Almighty Christ for our "battle bow" and through Him can be "more than conquerors." He has overcome the world (Jn. 16:33), and can give us the victory over it; over Satan and yes, over self, when we know Him in this way. We can say individually, "Christ is my Battle Bow!"

The Absolute Ruler: This describes Christ as to what He will be at His Second Advent to earth, the most absolute monarch and autocratic ruler the world has ever seen: "King of kings and Lord of lords." Being infinite in wisdom, He will require no councillors to assist Him in the administration of His kingdom. The judicial, legislative, and executive branches of government will be in His hands alone (see Isa. 33:22). Being infinite also in goodness and love, there will be no dangers when He possesses absolute power. As the Righteous and Holy One, He will exercise His prerogatives in perfect righteousness and holiness. He will exact from the nations the homage and acknowledgement of His claims which they now refuse to give Him. Oh! that they would now listen to His voice in Psalm 2:10-12.

Yet now we who are His should acknowledge Him as the Absolute Ruler of our lives. We should say, "Christ is my absolute Ruler!" Four precious titles of Christ—are we enjoying them in practice? Both Advents of our Saviour hold tremendous blessing for us when entered into, for He not only came once; He is just as surely coming again.

16
Are We Watching?

The Second Advent of Christ will catch the unsuspecting world with surprise and terrible destruction (1 Thess. 5:3) but no believer should be unaware of its approach: "Ye, brethren, are not in darkness, that that day should overtake you as a thief" (1 Thess. 5:4). Yet how many Christians are alert to the nearness of this great event? Do we actually realize the signs on the horizon that clearly indicate "the coming of the Lord draweth nigh" (Jas. 5:8)? John wrote, "The whole world lieth in [the Wicked One]" (1 Jn. 5:19) and it is fast asleep in his arms. But no believer should be, for we are exhorted to be morally and spiritually awake (1 Thess. 5:6-10).

Our Lord said, "Of that day and hour knoweth no man" (Mt. 24:36), yet in the same discourse He tells three parables that reveal the existence of signs prior to His return to earth. The parable of the fig tree (Mt. 24:32-33) which emphasizes the *fact* of signs; the second, about the days of Noah (Mt. 24:37-41) to demonstrate the *need* of signs, making the godly aware of His coming and arousing the unbelievers; the third of the householder (Mt. 24:42-44) to establish the *value* of signs that encourage us to watch.

It is the purpose of the Lord to awaken His people and guide them by these signs through the deceptive, dangerous days at the end; but it requires spiritual eyes and obedient hearts to discern His near return. Are we that awake today?

In addition, there are three special spheres of significant interest today, plainly declaring the approaching advent of our Lord, each of them foretold in the Word of God. They are the political realm, the moral realm, and the ecclesiastical realm.

1. *The Political Realm:* What a world of paradoxes we live in! Special efforts are made for world peace, but we constantly hear of "wars and rumors of wars." Excessive spending to preserve life and health, but billions spent for life's destruction. Increase of culture and refinement, yet never more barbarism. Astounding developments in education, but never greater moral blindness. Great efforts to produce unity among nations, yet producing less cohesion than ever! How will it all end?

The same question arose in the mind of Nebuchadnezzer centuries ago, "What shall be in the latter days?" Through Daniel, God revealed that immediately prior to the Second Advent of Christ, a world empire with a federation of ten kings would exist (Dan. 2:40-44; 7:23-28). It was also revealed to the apostle John (Rev. 17:12-14). Christ foretold the political conditions of the turbulent time prior to His coming (Mt. 24 & 25). His words of Matthew 24:4-8 seem descriptive of present-day chaos. Surely the disintegration of nations is definitely upon us, rapidly coming into the final phase of Gentile history when this federal empire under Satan will rule the world (Rev. 13). But do we see this approach?

2. *The Moral Realm:* The description of "the last days" is forcefully depicted by the apostle in 2 Timothy 3:1-5, where he records the abnormal times when iniquity will bring the return of the old evils of heathenism into the midst of Christendom. Every feature in this prophecy prevails today. Let us not close our eyes to these facts, for they definitely precede the advent of our coming Lord.

Paul also said that evil men and seducers from true godliness and right morals shall wax worse and worse, deceiving themselves and others (2 Tim. 3:13). Such men profess being enlightened and free men, but they only become darkened in their philosophies and enslaved in selfishness and sin, though claiming to be advancing. The rejection of God's Word for guidance can only increase the recession of men into moral darkness that becomes as heathenish as that of the ancient world!

In Revelation 9:20-21, the Seer describes the character and

conduct of human society at the end time prior to the Lord's return. *Murder* was going to be a common crime; how true that has become! They are no longer exceptional. Not only are they increasing in number but in the horrible way they are enacted.

Sorceries in the Greek is the word *pharmakia*, meaning "the administering of drugs" (*Thayer's* Lexicon) and this predominates today. The impure practice in the field of pharmacy has developed vice and sin, for it is not restricted to the useful sphere of health. Its illicit use now inflames the vilest of passions that rot away the moral fiber of human society, leading to that which is next linked with it:

Fornication. We see that society is now deluged with the subversion of the sanctity of marriage and its laws, for the sins of fornication and adultery have increasingly become a public feature of the social decay in the last days.

Dishonesty and *thefts* prevail everywhere, with complete disregard of others' rights, obliterating moral distinctions in order to practice fraud, theft, and deceit wherever possible. Do these facts declare the near Advent of Christ or not? Let God's Word speak to our hearts and consciences today.

3. *The Ecclesiastical Realm:* The New Testament contains serious warnings of the declining state of the church toward the end. "In the latter times some shall depart from the faith," drawn away by demonic influence. Cheating their own consciences, men become exponents of the teachings that have seduced them (1 Tim. 4:1-7). The apostle Peter confirms this in his second epistle also, chapter 2. The unfortunate tolerance and lack of conviction in Christians today increases this departure, though they themselves may not depart from the truth.

Jude traces this in three stages: "the way of Cain...the error of Balaam...the gainsaying of [Korah]" (Jude 11). God demands atonement through the blood of Christ, but many ecclesiastics follow Cain's bloodless sacrifice, leading many to perdition. True men and women of God willingly sacrifice position, wealth, and life for the sake of divine principles, but Balaam and his kind compromise principles for worldly position, wealth, and personal advantage. The final stage of this apostasy is in "the gainsaying of [Korah]," who, though a priest of God, stood up and publicly contended against the truth of God to his own destruction and that of his followers (Num. 16). Today in the highest places of Christendom, many boldly stand up and oppose the Word of God to teach what they claim is advanced learning. The Scriptures hold out no hope of a general recovery from these things and warn that at the end the churches will be in a state of declension (Rev. 2 & 3). It is more unfortunate that even true believers have "itching ears" and help multiply such teachers whose motive is only to please the ears and satisfy the taste of the people (2 Tim. 4:3-4).

In the light of this truth from God's Word, we must recognize that a strong ecumenical movement in Christendom will culminate in the final apostasy, following the Rapture of the Church (2 Thess. 2:1-3). The ultimate unity of all religions into one world system will come and accommodate the ideas of each constituent under the deception of the devil. Yet at the zenith of its ease and power, it will meet its doom. The political federation will destroy the religious systems that have so long deceived the world, thus fulfilling God's judgment (Rev. 17:16-17). In turn, the political power will be destroyed at the Lord's appearing (Rev. 19:11-21). Do we really observe these things coming, or are we asleep?

If these worldwide signs are fast developing toward their finality and the Lord's coming *to earth*, my beloved fellow-believer, how near are we then to the blessed hope that Christ will come for His true ones? Are we morally and spiritually awake? Do we show by our character and conduct in life now, that we are waiting for our Lord from heaven? Should we close our eyes to the evidences around us that were foretold in God's Word, and not live as those who wait for Him? God forbid! "Blessed are those servants, whom the Lord when He cometh shall find watching!" (Lk. 12:37). Then "let your loins be girded about, and your lights burning; and ye yourselves like unto men that wait for their Lord" (Lk. 12:35-36).

17
The Morning Star

> *"I Jesus have sent Mine angel to testify unto you these things in the churches. I am the root and offspring of David, and the bright and morning star"* (Revelation 22:16).

A threefold presentation of Christ is in this text, revealing glorious titles of our Lord in relation to the World, Israel and the Church: He is presented as "Jesus" to the world; a name that holds the possibility of eternal salvation for all, for it means "Saviour" (Mt. 1:21). How the world today needs the value of this Name, for "neither is there salvation in any other, for there is none other name under heaven given among men, whereby we must be saved." He is also presented as "the Root and Offspring of David" to Israel, the One who as David's Lord and David's Son (Ps. 110:1) will bring to fruition all the covenant promises of God to Israel. He alone will establish the godly remnant of Israel in the perpetual glory of their King and kingdom!

Then He is presented as "the Bright and Morning Star" to the Church, His blood-bought Bride. This is a title of special affection for the saints today, cheering our hearts and encouraging our spirits while the shadows of moral and spiritual apostasy deepen around us. There are only three Scriptures that give reference to this special title of our Lord and are worthy of our earnest consideration.

2 PETER 1:19

"We have also a more sure word of prophecy; whereunto ye

do well that ye take heed, as unto a light that shineth in a dark place until the day dawn, and the day star [morning star] arise in your hearts."

Two facts are herein revealed: first, the prophetic Word is like a lamp which lightens the moral and spiritual darkness of earth, exposing its corruption of evil everywhere. Yet all prophecy points to the dawn of a new day for the earth when our Lord Jesus Christ will appear in power and great glory.

Second, there is also revealed a daystar (or morning star), telling us much more! This tells my heart that the day of glory is nearing. This morning star is the harbinger of a new day, but the star shines *before* the dawn of that day in the midst of the darkness.

Though nothing of that glory is now visible to the eye, yet the morning star, brightly gleaming, sends its message of hope. Hallelujah! If the prophet's word fixes my hope and affections on Christ alone, rather than the dawn of that new day, then the daystar has arisen in my heart.

REVELATION 2:28

"And I will give him the morning star." In the letter to the church of Thyatira, the Lord reveals the sad conditions of spiritual evil. There is no promise given for power over the nations of the world. Instead, the Lord promises the overcomer this honor, "And I will give him the morning star!"

The glory and honor of the coming kingdom with its magnificence is not the complete satisfaction of the believer's heart, for there is a greater satisfaction than even the kingdom of glory—"the morning star," Christ Himself! What a blessed incentive is kingdom truth for the believer, but greater than that in the midst of ecclesiastical and moral darkness today is the glory of what Christ Himself is to the overcomer's heart. The Person of Christ alone can fully satisfy the heart.

> "Taken up with Thee, Lord Jesus, I would be;
> Finding joy and satisfaction all in Thee;
> Thou the nearest, and the dearest
> Unto me! unto me!"

REVELATION 22:16

As the Old Testament closes, it presents Christ as "the Sun of Righteousness" who will rise "with healing in His wings" (Mal. 4:2), chasing away the darkness, sorrow, pain, and sickness. The world will see that day (Rev. 1:7). The New Testament closes by presenting Christ as the bright morning star (Rev. 22:16), but the world will be asleep, and will never see the star (1 Thess. 5:5-6). It is the Church alone, His Bride, that can know Him as the Bright and Morning Star. He is to be known by us as such now, before He shines as the Son of Righteousness, for when the sun arises the stars go out! "Therefore let us not sleep, as do others; but let us watch and be sober" (1 Thess. 5:6).

Beloved, do you and I see Him as the Bright Morning Star? Are our hearts—in the midst of this world's darkness—fixed on Him alone? Dearer than all the glory of His coming kingdom is the blessed and lovely Person of Christ Himself; and if our hope and affections are on Him alone, then the day afar has arisen in our own hearts! The words of Gerhard Tersteegen (translated by Frances Beven) illumines this truth to us:

> *"Midst the darkness, storm, and sorrow, one bright gleam I see;*
> *Well I know the blessed morrow, Christ will come for me.*
> *Midst the light, and peace, and glory of the Father's home,*
> *Christ for me is watching, waiting, waiting, till I come.*
>
> *Who is this who comes to meet me on the desert way?*
> *As the Morning Star foretelling God's unclouded day?*
> *He it is who came to win me on the Cross of shame;*
> *In His glory well I know Him, evermore the same!"*

Before the shadows of great tribulation deepen in their intense blackness on the nations of this world, with the outpouring of God's wrath on this Christ-rejecting scene, you and I will have heard His glad shout (1 Thess. 4:13-18) and shall meet Him in the air above, to be forever with Himself and like Himself evermore. How satisfied we shall be: "I shall be satisfied, when I awake, with Thy likeness" (Ps. 17:15). Yet do not forget that also in that same moment, the Spirit of God will present to Christ an object suitable and worthy of His love forevermore, the Church,

His Bride, an object for the perfect satisfaction of His heart.

Surely then, we rejoice that for the world, for Israel, and especially for the Church, Christ Himself is the hope alone to set all things right at His blessed return. Thus may our hearts gladly give Him the place of the Bright Morning Star in our affection, enabling us to say, "Amen. Even so, come, Lord Jesus!"

18
What His Return Means to Me

The personal blessings of the Lord's return are more important than understanding all the mysteries of prophecy! What will His return mean to me personally?

1. *My trials of the wilderness journey will be ended.* The journey of the Ark of the Covenant began in the wilderness. Two staves were provided to carry it (Ex. 25:13-15), until its final resting place was reached; then they were removed (2 Chron. 5:1-9). The journey was finished. So will mine be finished at His return for "there remaineth...a rest for the people of God" (Heb. 4:9).

> *"And when we reach the further shore,*
> *Our perils and privations o'er—*
> *Rough seas behind, bright skies before;*
> *How we will bless the mighty hand*
> *Of Him who brought us safe to land."*

2. *My promised perfections will be realized* (Phil. 1:6; Ps. 138:8). I shall enjoy the perfection of my new body (Rom. 8:23)—"the dew of eternal youth" (Ps. 110:3; Phil. 3:20-21). I shall also have the perfection of Christ-like character (1 Jn. 3:2), and the perfection of spiritual vision: "We shall see Him as He is" (1 Jn. 3:2).

3. *My reunion with and recognition of all saints.* David expected to see his deceased child (2 Sam. 12:23). Saints will see Abraham, Isaac, and Jacob (Mt. 8:11). Paul looked forward to seeing his converts (1 Thess. 2:19-20). Peter, James and John recognized Moses and Elijah (Mt. 17:3). Personal identity will never disappear, and memory will be perfect (1 Cor. 13:12; Lk. 16:19-31).

4. *My knowledge and understanding will be perfect.* In the millennial kingdom, God says, "All shall know Me, from the least to the greatest" (Heb. 8:11). Today, my knowledge and understanding are partial, not complete; but when my Lord returns for me, through eternity I shall understand and clearly apprehend my Lord Jesus Christ. Until then, may I grow in grace and the knowledge of Him (2 Pet. 3:18).

5. *My devotion and service will be perfect:* "And His servants shall serve Him" (Rev. 22:3). My service will be without cessation, without weariness, without failure—in the joy and freedom of eternal love.

> "For doubt not that in the world above,
> There must be other offices of love.
> That other ministries and tasks there are—
> Sure it is written that His servants there
> Shall serve Him still."

6. *My reward will be graciously bestowed.* "What is my reward then?" Is there not the soul-winner's crown to gain, the crown of rejoicing? (1 Thess. 2:19-20); the crown of righteousness (2 Tim. 4:8); the crown of glory for faithful shepherds (1 Pet. 5:4); the incorruptible crown (1 Cor. 9:24-27); the martyr's crown (Rev. 2:10); and the nameless crown of Revelation 3:11-12. Let me be reminded of the exhortation, "Look to yourselves, that we lose not those things which we have wrought, but that we receive a full reward" (2 Jn. 8).

7. *My longing heart shall be satisfied.* "I shall be satisfied, when I awake with Thy likeness" (Ps. 17:15). Perfect and eternal satisfaction, and that forever!

> "There, Lord, to lose, in bliss of Thine embrace
> The recreant will;
> There, in the radiance of Thy blessed face,
> Be hushed and still;
> There, speechless at Thy pierced feet
> See none and nought beside,
> And know but this—that Thou art sweet,
> That I am satisfied."   (G. Tersteegen)

19
Raptured!

"The secret things belong unto the Lord our God," wrote Moses (Deut. 29:29). God does not reveal His "secret things" to the natural man for he is incompetent to understand them (1 Cor. 2:14). The natural eye, ear and heart can never receive the visions and the voices of the Spirit of God (1 Cor. 2:9). The incomprehensible realm of the Spirit is outside the range of human intelligence, in spite of the amazing wonders of man's scientific achievements. His discoveries are insignificant in contrast with the eternal energies and realities of the spiritual realm of the gospel.

There have been past events of divine manifestations that have been kept from the eyes of men, but revealed to spiritual hearts and minds. These events are samples of how God keeps the secrets of His power from the intelligence of men. But they also show what He does to reveal His mind to those who desire to know Him. Here are a few examples:

1. *Enoch's Translation* (Gen. 5:24; Heb. 11:5). Translated to heaven without passing through death, the mystery of this departure has never been explained by the world. It never will be; such a thing is inconceivable to human reasoning; but when you have the opportunity, you may ask Enoch—he was there!

2. *Elisha's Servant* (2 Ki. 6:8-23). Syrian hosts surrounded the city of Samaria by night and Elisha's servant was in great despair: "Alas, my master! How shall we do?" Elisha prayed, "Lord, I pray Thee, open his eyes, that he may see." Then he saw what the natural eye could not see and what the natural mind

could not know. God's "secret things" belong to Him and to whom the Spirit reveals them.

3. *Elijah's Translation* (2 Ki. 2:9-11). Elisha would never have seen the departure of his master to heaven had not the Spirit of God prepared him for this wonderful event. The "sons of the prophets" attempted to witness it, but were incapable. What did Elisha see? "A chariot and horses of fire"—the celestial conveyance to transport Elijah to heaven. He witnessed with spiritual eyes his master ascend to glory. The "sons of the prophets" made intensive search for Elijah but Elisha knew the search was hopeless. He had seen what none other saw, his master taken up by a whirlwind into heaven.

4. *Daniel's Vision* (Dan. 10:5-7). The glory of the celestial visitor was given for Daniel to see face to face; and to hear words that were like the voice of a multitude. The men with him saw nothing, terror falling on them as they hid themselves. "And I Daniel alone saw the vision," he declares. His companions could tell nothing of the event, other than the fact that they were terrified and fled. God has His ways of keeping His secrets from men as He reveals them to His own.

5. *Peter, James, and John* (Mt. 17:1-8). The glory of Christ's transfiguration on the Holy Mount was given only to three disciples; yet the face of the Lord shone with the brightness of the sun." The light was sufficient to light up the whole land, but did it? No! God kept it a secret from the eyes of the world and restricted the blessing of it to these three (see 2 Pet. 1:16-18).

6. *Resurrected Saints at the Time of the Crucifixion* (Mt. 27:1-53). The bodies of many saints arose when the Lord died, appearing in the Holy City to many after His Resurrection. Such an experience should have had a tremendous impact on the community, but, no, it was without public attention and known only to the participants and their friends. This was shrouded in secrecy and revealed only to the saints, a divine manifestation of God's power even in the darkness of Calvary.

7. *Stephen's Martyrdom* (Acts 7:44-60). Beloved and faithful Stephen, filled with the Holy Spirit and having his eyes fixed on heaven "saw the glory of God and Jesus standing [at] the right hand of God." None of the Jewish witnesses saw what he did,

nor could they. The murderous intent of their hearts and eyes had but one objective—the death of God's dear servant. What a comfort it was for Stephen to see God's glory and Jesus at His right hand at that moment! Praise God for such sights in crises!

8. *Saul's Conversion* (Acts 9:1-7). The glorified Lord arrested Saul on his journey to Damascus. He was the Lord's object of visitation and knew all that was taking place, not merely with his eyes and ears, but in the depths of his heart and conscience. There was no word for his companions. They had no sight of the glorified Lord and they were conscious only of an incomprehensible glare and sound (v. 7).

Likewise, if it was Paul who went up to Paradise (2 Cor. 12:1-4), no other person saw him go. The heavenly vision and revelation, which was unutterable in human language, was experienced by Paul alone. God continues to keep hidden from natural men His secrets.

9. *The Resurrection of Christ.* Without controversy, Christ's resurrection and His post-resurrection appearances are greater in scope than all our preceding examples. He came forth from the tomb of hewn stone that was surrounded by a guard of watchful soldiers, but none of them witnessed it. No human eye, nor ear, could share in that glory. His post-resurrection appearances were known only to "witnesses who were chosen of God" (Acts 10:40-41). He appeared in various guises to escape recognition (Lk. 24:15-16; Jn. 20:14-15), and He was able to vanish out of sight as he pleased (Lk. 24:31). For forty days on the earth the resurrected Saviour manifested Himself without the world ever seeing Him!

10. *The Rapture of the Saints* (1 Thess. 4:15-17). The coming of our Lord for His saints is definitely to be hidden from the eyes of the world and is outside the range of the natural man who is totally unable to comprehend its truth. It will be an event that is unprecedented for magnitude, when millions of resurrected saints and living saints shall be transported "in a moment, in the twinkling of an eye" by divine power, to "meet the Lord in the air" and to be forever in His Father's glory. Suddenly, without warning; silently, without commotion; secretly, without publicity—God will take all His own to glory! When? Perhaps today!

Out in the world—the darkness gathering quickly;
Peace is far off; men's hearts are full of fear;
Within the veil—God's children rest in safety,
They know their Lord's return is very near.

Out in the world—internal strife and warfare;
Kingdoms declining; bloodshed, loss and pain;
Within the veil—Christ's Church, just watching, praying,
Thrilled with His promise, "I will come again."

(Ivy M. Fordham)

The Rapture (1 Thess. 4:16-17) will be a fivefold event of matchless glory. The "blessed hope" will be consummated by an act of divine omnipotence beyond the finite understanding of the human mind. What will it involve for the saints?

1. *Caught away:* We shall be snatched away, "in a moment, in the twinkling of an eye" from this world, taken out of all distress of soul and body (2 Cor. 5:2, 4); out of all persecution and oppression; out of the entire sphere of sin and death. It is "the day of redemption" (Eph. 4:30; Rom. 8:23), not from the penalty of sin but from the presence of it entirely. It will be an act of divine grace freeing us from all sin; an act of divine mercy (Jude 21), freeing us from all misery.

2. *Caught up:* "Caught up *together*" for the "dead in Christ" and the living saints will be united; all members of the Body of Christ with their Head at that same moment. He will present His Church to "Himself" (Eph. 5:27), to perfect the glory of the Body (Eph. 1:23). On this occasion, for the first time the Church of all times and all lands will be with one another! Millions of saints, from Pentecost to the Rapture, will soar upwards together by the power of God and fill the heavenly regions with their Hallelujahs—the only ecumenical movement that will work!

3. *Transfigured:* This "body of humiliation" will be changed into a body of glory (Phil. 3:21). The corruptible body once planted in the grave will put on incorruption. The mortal ones will put on immortality (1 Cor. 15:51, 53). To the Lord's body of glory ours will be conformed (1 Cor. 15:49). The earthly body the soul dominates, but the heavenly body the spirit will dominate. It is called a "spiritual body" (1 Cor. 15:44-46). Perfect spirituali-

ty will control the new body. It will be in unrestricted dependence at the disposal of the spirit, a perfect instrument of the perfected life—indescribable in the splendor it will possess.

4. *Triumphant:* There will be victory when "in the air." For the air is the headquarters of Satan and his hosts of evil; there they rule over the darkness of this world (Eph. 6:12). Satan is called "the prince of the power of the air" (Eph. 2:2). Yet in the region of Satan's power, the headquarters of our enemies, there takes place the meeting of the Great Conqueror and His victorious saints. It is the Saviour's and our complete victory over the great foe. Read the description of this same event in 1 Corinthians 15:51-58, and you will understand the words of triumph in verse 57, "But thanks be to God which giveth us the victory through our Lord Jesus Christ." The victorious saints, as they rise to meet the Lord, sing a dual anthem of triumph: "O death, where is thy sting? O grave, where is thy victory?" (1 Cor. 15:55).

5. *Consummation:* "And so shall we ever [always] be with the Lord" (1 Thess. 4:17). Then the precious promise of the Lord will be finally fulfilled, "If I go…, I will come again and receive you unto Myself, that where I am, there ye may be also" (Jn. 14:3). We shall never leave His presence, never stray from His side. Always near to *Him!* Then will be perfect service and devotion: "His servants shall serve Him" (Rev. 22:3). Then there will be perfect worship and adoration: "And they shall see His face" (Rev. 22:4). Then we shall bear His perfect likeness: "And His name shall be on their foreheads" (Rev. 22:4). Surely "the Spirit and the Bride say, Come" (Rev. 22:17). The longing heart responds: "Even so, come, Lord Jesus" (Rev. 22:20).

> *"Lord Jesus, I am waiting, waiting Thy dear face to see:*
> *Resting on Thy promise, Thou shalt come again for me:*
> *Joy of Thy returning, wondrous meeting in the air,*
> *Wonder of all wonders, I'll be there!"* (David Penman)

Truly beloved, it is marvelous grace to know that we shall participate in this wonderful event that is hidden from the world—the secrecy of the Rapture! What love and grace!

The rapidity and the greatness of the Rapture should be a constant anticipation in our hearts. It will take place "in a moment; in the twinkling of an eye."

1. *Consider its rapidity.* Significantly, the word "moment" is the Greek word *atomos,* found only in 1 Corinthians 15:52. It is defined as "that which cannot be cut in two, undivided, indivisible." This is no longer true, for the atom has been split, producing fear of a possible world destruction.

Yet the Holy Spirit uses this word to indicate the rapidity of the Rapture of the saints. It will be accomplished "in a moment." The time element of this event is indivisible to the human mind. "The twinkling of an eye" has been calculated as the quickest, automatic action of the human body. Our departure from earth will be quicker than all speeds achieved by man; and also soundless! The Lord Himself confirms this in Revelation 22:20, "Behold, I come quickly."

2. *Consider its vastness.* It is not a solitary Enoch or Elijah being translated, but untold myriads "snatched up, to meet the Lord in the air." All the dead saints are to be resurrected: "And the dead shall be raised incorruptible" (1 Cor. 15:52). No selective group of saints, but all the righteous dead from Abel and onwards—"They that are Christ's at His coming" (1 Cor. 15:23). The Old Testament saints are His as well as New Testament believers. Who can deny this?

The words of 1 Corinthians 15:23 reveal a wide and comprehensive truth, telling that the graves of earth will be emptied of all the saints. The sea also will give up the precious dust of the redeemed. Then together with living saints all shall rise upward, not one missing. From all quarters of the earth brought together in a moment! How interesting to read Hebrews 11:39, which declares of Old Testament saints, "that they without us should not be made [complete]." Surely they will not be left in their disembodied state at our glorious resurrection! Why should they not join in the heavenly worship of the Lamb who redeemed them, and sing with us, "Thou art worthy" (Rev. 5). Dwell on the vastness of this event—numberless myriads meeting the Lord in the air and "in a moment."

Midst the darkness, storm and sorrow, one bright gleam I see:
Well I know, the blessed morrow, Christ will come for me.

20
From Groans to Glory

The doctrinal section of Romans extends from chapter 1 through chapter 8. Two distinct themes are given by the Spirit of God: God's justification of a sinner (1-5:11); and God's deliverance of a saint (5:12-8:39). The last section can be subdivided as follows: deliverance of a saint from sin's power (5:12-6:23); deliverance of a saint from the law (7:1-8:10); the complete deliverance of a saint from sin's presence—at death or at the Rapture by the "redemption of the body" (8:11-30); the blessed conclusion as the theme of our eternal praise (8:31-39). Until final deliverance, the groans of creation will be heard on every hand, but when the Lord comes, they will vanish away.

1. *The sufferings of this present time.* Suffering today is inevitable. Sin is the cause and the whole human race is subjected to sickness, sorrow, grief, and pain; each one in our own measure feeling sin's effect. Christians are also called on to suffer for Christ during His rejection by the world. Yet, though this is our present time for sufferings, God has the final answer for His children—glory! "For I reckon that the sufferings of this present time are not worthy to be compared with the coming glory to be revealed to us" (Rom. 8:18, JND Trans.).

God reveals three depths of human suffering in Exodus 3:7. There is suffering that is *seen:* "I have surely seen the affliction of My people." We see much of this around us, but God sees all. There is suffering that is deeper; it is *felt* though perhaps unseen: "I have heard their cry." God realizes this by the outpoured words of the lips expressing the inner feelings of the heart. But the suffering that is deepest, unseen and unuttered, lies deep in the sufferer's heart. Yet God says, "I *know* their sorrows." Whatever the depth of it and by whatever channel—spiritual, mental or physical—God knows; God loves; God cares!

2. *The groans of this present time.* Within Romans 8, from verses 22 to 26, we hear three kinds of groans:

a) The groans of creation: "The whole creation groaneth and travaileth in pain together until now" (v. 22). The literal creation (other than man) became subject to vanity—to death, but not willingly (v. 20). Creation is neither in its original creation nor in its final condition. It is a groaning creation, all out of adjustment, manifesting that all is in discord between earth and heaven. It groans, for "All the voices of nature are in the minor key" because of the sin of man.

b) The groans of the Christian: "Even we ourselves, who have the firstfruits of the Spirit, we also ourselves groan within ourselves, waiting for the adoption" (v. 23). Suffering saints are in pain, grief, and sorrow everywhere, their groans expressing the longing for final deliverance. Exercised and concerned believers look across the world of political, ecclesiastical, and moral chaos and groan with deep yearning for that deliverance which the coming of the Lord will bring.

c) The groans of the Holy Spirit: "The Spirit [Him]self makes intercession for us with groanings which cannot be uttered" (v. 26). No believer is able to comprehend the unspeakable sorrow and suffering in the world, nor the immensity of the great need around us, because of our infirmities. "We know not what to pray for as we ought," and how often in our emergencies we realize this. But here is where the Spirit of God in His power comes in to meet the need, praise God! He takes up our weaknesses and makes intercession *for us* according to God's perfect will and understanding (v. 27). He shares our longing. As long ago He "brooded upon the face of the waters" (Gen. 1:2) over a past chaotic scene, so today, where human limitations are unable to express the immensity of the need, the Spirit of God can and does minister as the perfect Advocate.

3. *The time of deliverance.* There is a day on God's calendar of events when the Almighty will say, "Enough!" The long night of

weeping will give way to the everlasting day of joy.

a) For the creation: it will be at "the manifestation of the sons of God" (Rom. 8:19). "The creature shall be set free from the bondage of corruption into the liberty of the glory of the children of God" (Rom. 8:21, JND Trans.). Creation fell when man did (Gen. 3:17-19). It shall be restored when man is, and then be no longer subject to vanity. The day of creation's emancipation will take place when the Lord Jesus Christ comes to set up His kingdom. (See Isa. 11:6-9; 35:1-2; 55:13; 65:25.) This is the "hope" of the literal creation (Rom. 8:19-20).

b) For the Christian: The creation groans and the Christian groans, for both are looking for that which will bring each into right relation to the other. The Christian is "waiting for the adoption, that is, the redemption of our body" (Rom. 8:23). This will be at the coming of the Lord, "who shall transform our body of humiliation into conformity to His body of glory, according to the working of the power which He has even to subdue all things to Himself" (Phil. 3:21. JND Trans.). What a blessed prospect. Nearer than ever! (Rom. 13:11-12).

c) For the Spirit of God: His groans for us will also be over. He knows that the end is certain and the purposes of God all center in His beloved Son. He knows that Christ is to be "the Firstborn among many brethren" (v. 29), the Head of a new race of beings. But in that time, He will be surrounded by those who shall bear His image, too. He knows that the saints are "predestinated to be conformed to the image of His Son" (v. 29). You can believe with all your soul in the predestination of saints. (Note Eph. 1:5; Rom. 8:29-30; Eph. 1:11) The truth always refers to saints alone. So certain is the Spirit of God about the purposes of God that He has written, "Whom He has foreknown...He has predestinated...He has called...He has justified and these also He has glorified." He already sees it as if it were, fulfilled.

4. *Our present consolation in suffering.* It is often true, as previously stated: "We do not know what we should pray for as we ought," but what a blessed antithesis between the words, "we know not" of verse 26 and the words, "we do know" in verse 28: "But we do know that all things work together for good to those who love God, to those who are called according to purpose"

(JND Tran.). God is making all things work together for the good of His people for they are under His control. The Spirit knows this and so should we.

Furthermore, what three triumphant challenges the believer can confidently make: "Who can be against us?" (Rom. 8:31). "Who is he that condemneth?" (Rom. 8:34). "Who shall separate us?" (Rom. 8:35). The purposes of our God for His beloved Son and all the redeemed saints belonging to Him, are marching forward to a blessed and eternal conclusion. Our deliverance is sure: we are going from groans to glory. Blessed deliverance! May it be soon.

> *"The whole creation groans, and waits to hear that voice,*
> *That shall restore her comeliness, and make her wastes rejoice.*
> *Come, Lord, and wipe away the curse, the sin, the stain,*
> *And make this blighted world of ours Thine own fair world again.*
> *'Come, then, Lord Jesus, Come.'"* (Horatius Bonar)

21
Every Eye Shall See Him

"Behold! He cometh with clouds; and every eye shall see Him, and they also which pierced Him; and all kindreds of the earth shall wail because of Him. Even so, Amen" (Revelation 1:7).

The subject and contents of the great book of Revelation are expressed by the opening words: "the Revelation of Jesus Christ" (1:1). They imply "the revealing, the manifestation, the appearing, of Jesus Christ." He Himself is the great center and subject of the book, in particular concerning His coming administration of judgment and glory. It is not merely Jesus Christ doing the revealing, but Jesus Christ being revealed to mortal view. Our verse is the great prophetic theme of the book, declaring in a few comprehensive words, the subject and purpose of the whole treatise:

1. *The inevitable fact of His coming:* "Behold! He cometh." The coming of Christ in His power and glory was the first prophecy preached by man (see Jude 14-15); and since that time the promises of Scripture concerning it have been abundant. The opening statement of our verse is only a re-stating of the great doctrine, confirming the whole body of divine truth. It is inevitable.

2. *The special manner of His coming:* "With clouds." The clouds of old were the well-known symbol of Jehovah's presence with His people (Ex. 13:21; 40:34-38), but Christ is coming *in* the clouds (Mk. 13:26), *with* them (Rev. 1:7), and *on* them (Mt. 24:30, JND Trans.). They are the symbols of His majesty (Ps. 18:9-12;

see also Dan. 7:13). What a sight in the heavens this will be as He descends with many diadems upon His head and clothed in regal splendor, saints and angels swelling His triumph in clouds of glory also.

3. *The publicity of His coming:* "And every eye shall see Him." This is a literal and a universal fact. There never has been and there never will be a human being who shall not see Him. To everyone that has lived and to everyone that shall live, He will reveal Himself and every eye will be compelled to meet His eye. When the great book of Revelation shall be historically fulfilled, every human being from the beginning to the end of time will have stood face to face with the Lord Jesus Christ—whether sinner or saint!

The dead shall be brought to life and they shall see Him. The living shall stand before Him (2 Tim. 4:1). The good and the wicked shall see Him; the great and the small shall see Him (1 Thess. 4:13-18; Mt. 25:31-46; Rev. 20:11-15). When the final purpose of God establishes His eternally new creation (Rev. 21:1-5), every human being will have met Jesus Christ face to face, eye to eye, either for eternal blessing or for eternal judgment. How deeply solemn is this fact.

4. *The particular distinction for some at His coming:* "And they which pierced Him." Though it will be a universal manifestation, yet a distinction that warns of impending disaster is indicated for some. His murderers will see Him face to face. Judas, the betrayer of Christ, has yet to face Him! The soldiers who mocked Him, buffeted Him, spat upon Him, and crowned Him with thorns; the priests who unjustly condemned Him and the soldier who pierced His blessed side, all will again see Him! The rabble mob that vehemently and hatefully cried, "Away with Him! Crucify Him!" will see Him again and face to face. Pilate also, who wrongfully commanded Him to be crucified, will face Him, and the question of his heart will not be: "What shall I then do with Jesus?" but, "What will He do with me?" Yes, all who to the end of time have wronged, persecuted, wounded, insulted, and rejected Him, will be compelled to face Him in judgment and gaze upon Him whom they have pierced, both Jew and Gentile alike. It is inevitable. There is a day of reckoning for all

of humanity in respect to their attitude and conduct toward the Person of the Son of God.

5. *The universal mourning at His appearing:* "And all kindreds of the earth shall wail because of Him." The effect of His return will be a universal one, not restricted to any particular portion of the world, but undoubtedly reaching into every part of the globe where mankind is found. No nation, nor any individual, will be excepted from it.

a) The godly remnant of Israel, in repentance, shall mourn. The occasion will be the time of Israel's last conflict with the nations of the Gentiles, and also will be their deliverance (Zech. 12:1-9). In that day, Jerusalem will be an intoxicating cup of divine judgment for the nations (see Isa. 51:21-23); the nations will drink of that cup, stagger and fall, never to rise again (Dan. 2:44-45). That day will be one of unprecedented trouble and suffering for Israel, but the godly remnant shall be delivered (Jer. 30:7). It will be Israel's greatest spiritual crisis (Zech. 12:10-14), and also it will be God's final triumph over them. The godly remnant, pouring out their great national confession (Isa. 53), will find their Messiah alone can and will comfort them (Isa. 61:2-3) in that great national day of atonement (Zech. 13:1-6).

b) The ungodly of all the world shall also mourn. The appearing of Jesus Christ is hated by the ungodly (2 Pet. 3:3-7) for it will end forever their sinful pleasures. It will turn their self-confidence into fear and consternation (1 Thess. 5:3). It will change their sinful songs of mirth and merriment into shrieks of horror and despair, causing them to hide in the dens and the rocks of the mountains in fear (Rev. 6:16-17). His appearing will bring the terrors of judgment upon them and not a family, tribe, or nation shall escape.

The minuteness and the perfection of this judgment has been solemnly stated by the Lord Jesus, Himself, "The Son of Man shall send forth His angels, and they shall gather out of His kingdom all things that offend, and them that do iniquity; and shall cast them into a furnace of fire; there shall be wailing and gnashing of teeth" (Mt. 13:41-42). The angelic bureau of investigation will effect the apprehension of every offender and the removal from this world of all things that offend the holy character of God and of His coming King, our Lord and Saviour Jesus Christ.

Pause! Reflect on the seriousness and thoroughness of this universal judgment in that coming day. The present increasing worldwide violence and corruption, together with every individual offender, will receive inevitable judgment and sudden destruction. Can we take it in? Its scope and thoroughness is solemnly stated by the words of Jesus. May we visualize clearer than ever what is to happen to this sin-loving and Christ-rejecting world. It will move us to seek to snatch many from the fire by His grace (Jude 23).

6. *The believer's ratification of His appearing:* "Even so, Amen." The believer can only say, "So be it." Following the centuries and millennia of longsuffering and patience, God's day of inevitable judgment must fall; the lowliest believer can but say, "This is right." There is a twofold lesson for the believer in all this. For the believer, His coming shines as "the morning star." It is "the blessed hope" for the saint, telling us that, instead of coming judgment, we "wait for His Son from heaven...even Jesus, our deliverer from the coming wrath" (see 1 Thess. 1:10; Phil. 3:20-21). We long to see His face (1 Jn. 3:2), and we cry with heartfelt longings, "Even so, come, Lord Jesus" (Rev. 22:20).

For the unsaved, His coming spells eternal tragedy, the inevitable retribution and eternal judgment that is inescapable (Jude 14-15). Are not the clouds of coming judgment appearing on the horizon of this world's history more than ever? They are accumulating with intensity every day. The most tragic day in world history for the unbeliever looms on the horizon now!

Beloved reader, which will be your portion then—blessing or judgment? If you are not saved, come to a waiting Saviour who welcomes all sinners who will trust in His precious blood to redeem from sin (Mt. 11:28; Jn. 6:37; Eph 1:7).

22
The Last Wedding

The first wedding (Gen. 2:21-3:7) ended in failure, but the last one will not! It will have a perfect Bridegroom and a perfect Bride, being consummated in a perfect place—heaven (Rev. 19:6-9). For once, they really will live happily ever after.

1. *The glorious Bridegroom:* Contrary to earthly custom, pre-eminence will be given to the Bridegroom. The event is called "The marriage of the Lamb." Is it not written, "that in all things He might have the pre-eminence"? (Col. 1:18). It is His joy that is especially in view, not ours. The marriage reveals the secret of Ephesians 5:32, that the Church of the New Testament is to be His Bride. He has loved the Church with a deathless and unchangeable love, a love always active, not resting until He presents it to Himself in glory (Eph. 5:25-27). More of the oil of gladness will be poured upon His head than upon ours (Heb. 1:9). What a moment of joy it will be for Him when "He shall see of the travail of His soul and shall be satisfied" (Isa. 53:11).

2. *His glorious Bride:* "His wife hath made herself ready" (Rev. 19:7). Did you know that believers must make themselves ready for this glorious occasion? Each spot, wrinkle, blemish, or any such thing must be removed (Eph. 5:27). This precedes the wedding, for our lives have to be reviewed at the Bema, the Judgment Seat of Christ. "The light of the Throne will be cast over and upon every moment of our lives, discovering the hidden, and bringing out the true character of act, word, and service. The enigmas of life will be explained, unsolved problems cleared up, and all mistakes and misunderstandings rectified.

We appear before the Bema of Christ crowned and glorified—"raised in glory" (1 Cor. 15:43), to have the light of the Throne cast upon our past. What a mercy this is so. We shall then pass from the Bema with its searching light into the presence of the Lamb as His Bride and wife forever," writes Walter Scott.

"To her was granted that she should be arrayed in fine linen, clean and white; for the fine linen is the righteousnesses of the saints." The fine linen, pure and beautiful, represents her righteous acts done on earth, which were done by the power of the Holy Spirit (See Jn. 16:13-14). Her deeds will have been appraised at their true value in heaven. She is arrayed in them, expressing the words, "She hath made herself ready." Then she will pass from the Bema into the loved presence of the Lamb as His Bride for the marriage, a glorious Church "not having spot, or wrinkle, or any such thing, but...holy and without blemish" (Eph. 5:27).

What grace this is! The Bride not only has the righteousness of Christ, by which she is accounted righteous before God, but the personal acts of her deeds done on earth for His glory, contribute to the beauty of the wedding robes for the Bridegroom's joy. Beloved, what are we doing now to weave the bridal robes we shall wear in heaven at the marriage? Only while on earth can this be done before He comes.

Notice too the Bride's eternal beauty. Her bridal glory never fades! After the millennium, when the new heaven and new earth appears (Rev. 21), she arrives at the center of that new universe "as a bride adorned for her husband." An eternal marriage of the eternal Bridegroom and His Bride, the Church, never to lose their bridal glory! May it be very soon when we hear Him say, "Rise up, my love, my fair one, and come away" (Song of Sol. 2:10).

> *"A little while"—Come, Saviour, Come!*
> *For Thee Thy Bride has waited long;*
> *Oh, take Thy wearied pilgrims home,*
> *To sing the new eternal song.*
> *To see Thy glory, and to be*
> *In every thing conformed to Thee."*

23
Thy Kingdom Come

The hope of the Church does not terminate with the marriage of the Lamb, for immediately after it will be the punishment of the high ones in the heavens, and the kings of the earth (Isa. 24:21). Then the kingdom will be given to His "little flock" (Lk. 12:32). Daniel wrote, "The saints of the Most High shall take the kingdom" (7:18). John said, "I saw thrones, and they sat upon them" (Rev. 20:4). The saints who will have been at the Judgment Seat of Christ and are adjudged worthy, will be made the judges of the world, the ruling aristocracy of the kingdom (1 Cor. 6:2; 2 Pet. 1:11). As glorified saints, they will reign as kings, with Christ their Head, over worlds forever (Rev. 22:5). The promise of God is: "glory in the Church by Christ Jesus throughout all ages, world without end. Amen" (Eph. 3:21). The coming kingdom will be in two phases: first, the millennial kingdom; second, the eternal kingdom. Let us briefly consider them.

THE MILLENNIAL KINGDOM

Its duration: "They shall be priests of God and of Christ, and shall reign with Him a thousand years" (Rev. 20:6). To spiritualize this Scripture is error, for the literal interpretation is imperative. The expression, "a thousand years," is stated six times in Revelation 20:2-7. First, Satan is bound for that period. Second, nations will not be deceived during that time. Third, martyred saints will reign through it. Fourth, the rest of the dead do not live until it is ended. Fifth, all in the first resurrection will reign with Christ. Sixth, Satan will be loosed after this period (v. 7).

Its nature: The Old Testament is saturated with its details. Major and minor prophets tell of its glory. Revelation 20 is not entirely silent of its government. Three expressions characterize the kingdom: *"Judgment"* will be given the enthroned saints (v. 4). All shall be *priests* of God (v. 6). They shall *reign* also (v. 6). Judicial, priestly, and kingly activity will be ours! Contrary to present desires for the complete separation of church and state, this disappears in the kingdom. Tenderness and severity combine to rule in perfect balance (see Isa. 40:10-11). It will be "the times of the restitution of all things" spoken of by Peter (Acts 3:20-21). What a glorious kingdom, and to be shared in God's great mercy and grace by His saints!

THE ETERNAL KINGDOM

Its duration: After the final rebellion (Rev. 20:7-10), and the final judgment (Rev. 20:11-15), will come the final kingdom of our Lord and Saviour, Jesus Christ (2 Pet. 1:11). Then we shall reign "for ever and ever" (Rev. 22:5). It will be the universal kingdom of God, perpetuated forever; all sin banished, a new and eternal world. It will end the first Creation and be the beginning of the "new creation" as stated by Paul in 1 Corinthians 15:24-28. The giving up of the kingdom by Christ to the Father does not mean the end of our Lord's regal activity, but from here onward the unity of the Godhead is seen in the eternal kingdom, when "God may be all in all." There will then be one throne: "the throne of God and of the Lamb" (Rev. 22:3).

Its nature: "Behold, I make all things new," says the Lord (Rev. 21:5). New and perfect conditions! Two can be mentioned specifically. First, perhaps the greatest, "the tabernacle of God is with men, and He will dwell with them, and they shall be His people, and God Himself shall be with them, and be their God" (Rev. 21:3).

Second, the most familiar things in life today will be absent. "No more death; neither sorrow; neither shall there be any more crying; nor pain: for the former things are passed away" (Rev. 21:4).

Today, in the hour of despair or discouragement, the words of our Saviour should never be forgotten, His last words to us.

They will give us courage and strength: "Behold, I come quickly"; again, "Behold, I come quickly"; and again, "Surely I come quickly!"(Rev. 22:7, 12, 20).

It is the Christian who alone has confidence and assurance that a righteous kingdom will yet appear on the earth. Did not our Lord instruct His disciples to pray, "Thy kingdom come. Thy will be done, in earth, as it is in heaven"? (Mt.6:10). Today the Lord's people should pray even more fervently: "Thy kingdom come!" The words are found in the first prayer the Lord taught, and in substance they are quoted at the end of the Bible when the Apostle John responded to the Lord's statement of His soon return, by praying, "Even so, come, Lord Jesus" (Rev. 22:20). "The kingdoms of this world" are yet to be "the kingdoms of our Lord, and of His Christ" according to Revelation 11:15.

Christ will be the Ruler: "And the Lord shall be King over all the earth" (Zech. 14:9). Human efforts to establish social and political improvements on earth have been unsuccessful. The prophetic Word declares that the future kingdom of God on the earth will be centered in an indispensable Person—God's chosen King (Ps. 2:6). It will be a personal ruler who will stand between God and men in the day of His kingdom. The world does not primarily need a better philosophy of government or better laws of legislation, but only a Person, who has character, wisdom and power to rule for God among men. That Man, that Person is Christ! Let us indeed pray earnestly, "Thy kingdom come!"

Christ's names and titles qualify Him to rule: both in His humanity and deity.

1. His Human Name. Isaiah reveals Him as One who will reign in righteousness and names Him "a Man" (Isa. 32:1-2). The prophet Daniel, in his glorious vision of Christ's coming kingdom, describes His appearance as "one like the Son of Man" (Dan. 7:13-14). All of His earthly experiences testify to His perfect knowledge of men and their needs. His life, His sorrows, His privations, His sufferings, and His death, all declare His perfect humanity, so that in the day of His kingdom, He will be a human King—a perfect Man!

2. His Divine Name. It is equally true that the coming King is

more than a man! "His name shall be called Immanuel, that is, God with us (Isa. 7:14; Mt. 1:23). No greater cluster of divine titles can be found than in Isaiah 9:6, "Wonderful, Counselor, the Mighty God, the everlasting Father, the Prince of Peace." The Lord even identifies Himself and His deity in Isaiah 44:6, "Thus saith Jehovah, the King of Israel, and His Redeemer, Jehovah of Hosts; I am the First and I am the Last, and beside Me there is no God."

His character qualifies Him to rule: "Behold My Servant...in whom My soul delighteth" (Isa. 42:1). All other rulers, even the best, have been imperfect in character. What a sharp contrast with Christ! Righteousness shall be the girdle of His loins, and faithfulness the girdle of His reins" (Isa. 11:5). His holy character in the kingdom is described by Isaiah, "For great is the Holy One of Israel in the midst of thee" (Isa. 12:6). In Psalm 24, note the One who alone is the King of Glory, worthy to go through "the everlasting doors" into the kingdom.

His ability qualifies Him to rule: His ability is perfect. In the face of internal distress and external danger, He will prove competent to correct all political, economic, moral, and physical problems. Of Him it is written, "He shall not fail nor be discouraged, till He have set judgment in the earth: and the isles shall wait for His law" (Isa. 42:4). The administration of His kingdom will be perfect when the eyes of all "see the King in His beauty," ruling in righteousness (Isa. 33:17).

His ability to control the judicial branch of His government is perfect. "For the Lord is our Judge," wrote Isaiah (33:22). Though saints and angels will be under His judicial authority, yet He will be the director and head, final authority and control of the Department of Justice.

His ability to control the legislative branch of His government is perfect. "For the Lord is our...lawgiver" (Isa. 33:22). You may read the Constitution of His kingdom in Matthew 5, 6, and 7. The laws of His coming kingdom are recorded there in the so-called Sermon on the Mount. The administration of those laws will be under His control and authority, as indicated by the oft-spoken expression, "I say unto you." His laws must be and will be obeyed by all!

His ability to control the executive branch of His government is perfect. "For the Lord is our...King," (Isa. 33:22). Christ Himself will be the Chief Executive of the government during His worldwide kingdom. By His own person and power will He reign and exercise the authority of His monarchy. A true and righteous King indeed! "Behold, a king shall reign in righteousness," said the prophet (Isa. 32:1).

How remarkable is this prophetic forecast of His kingdom, naming even the divisions of modern government, the judicial, the legislative, and the executive branches of government. We look forward today with joyful anticipation for the King to come and claim His kingdom, setting up His earthly throne and exercising His kingly rule. For in that day, not only will there be many other blessed facts about His reign, but how touching are the words of the prophet when he adds concerning that kingdom and its blessings, "The inhabitant shall not say, I am sick; the people that dwell therein shall be forgiven their iniquity" (Isa. 33:24).

Then "why speak ye not a word of bringing the King back?" (2 Sam. 19:10) Shall we not fervently pray, "Thy kingdom come!"

> *Lift up your heads! Events are moving fast!*
> *The trump we soon may hear:*
> *One moment's space and we shall all have passed*
> *Beyond this troubled sphere.*
>
> *Lift up your heads—yea, lift them up and sing*
> *With heart, and mind, and voice:*
> *For any day now, we may see the King.*
> *Look up! Expect! Rejoice!*

24
The Glories of Heaven

The glories of heaven are revealed by the Spirit of God in Revelation 4 & 5. The outline divisions of this book are given us in 1:19, as John is commanded to "write therefore what thou hast seen, and the things that are, and the things that are about to be after these" (JND Trans.). The Revelation therefore has a threefold division: First, "what thou hast seen," covered by the glorious vision described in chapter 1 concerning the Son of Man; the second, "the things that are," recorded in chapters 2 and 3, giving a spiritual or prophetic history of the Church during the present age; third, "the things which shall be hereafter," found from chapter 4 to the end of the book.

Therefore, between the end of chapter 3 and the commencement of the heavenly glories revealed in chapter 4, we can safely assume on the authority of Scripture that the saints of this age will have been raptured to be "forever with the Lord" before the "hour of trial" (Rev. 3:10) comes upon the whole world. The following Scriptures reveal this event: John 14:1-3; 1 Corinthians 15:51-52; 1 Thessalonians 1:10; 4:13-18; 5:1-10—all implying the translation of the saints before the judgments of God commence. How it is vividly illustrated by John's own translation in the vision, to heaven, a voice commanding him, "Come up hither." From heaven, John then sees all the unfolding of heaven's glory and God's wrath poured on the earth, even as the glorified saints shall also (Rev. 4:1-2).

The fourth and fifth chapters particularly reveal for our blessing and encouragement, the glories of heaven that shall meet our eyes when we have been raptured to glory at the coming of the Lord for His saints. What John saw in the Apocalyptic vision we shall see! The glories of heaven shall begin unfolding themselves to our wondering eyes as soon as we are there! But let us seek to enjoy a sweet foretaste of them by the help of the Spirit of God (1 Cor. 2:9-10), as we meditate together upon God's precious Word.

THE GLORY OF THE THRONE

The immediate glory reaching our gaze as we enter this heavenly scene is the glory of the throne: "Behold, a throne was set in heaven" (4:2). It is the throne of the Eternal, "high and lifted up" (Isa. 6:1), undoubtedly the highest pinnacle of the universe of God. It stands firm, immovable, and secure, for the attacks of Satanic hosts and evil men cannot move this throne. When the kingdoms of earth are shaken, God's throne and kingdom stand firm. "Wherefore, we receiving a kingdom which cannot be moved, let us have grace, whereby we may serve God acceptably with reverence and godly fear" (Heb. 12:28).

This glorious throne is occupied by One that "to look upon was like a jasper and a sardine (sardius) stone." This limited description of the Occupant implies the impossibility of human intelligence to define the glory of God. Even the Apostle Paul wrote that he was caught up into paradise, and "heard unspeakable things said, which it is not allowed to man to utter" (2 Cor. 12:4; JND Trans.). The jasper is a precious stone, crystalline and purple in color, perhaps a symbol of the glorious rule of God; and the sardius, of fiery red appearance, is perhaps the symbol of divine justice and punitive righteousness which God is about to pour out from heaven to the earth. His infinite glory and judicial wrath are both connected with His throne in the book of Revelation.

Yet surrounding the throne is an emerald rainbow, reminding us that mercy and grace are still divine attributes of God's being, a truth that will never be forgotten through eternity by the redeemed saints, even when they shall gaze upon the glory of God. Even then we shall still sing of His amazing grace.

24
The Glories of Heaven

The glories of heaven are revealed by the Spirit of God in Revelation 4 & 5. The outline divisions of this book are given us in 1:19, as John is commanded to "write therefore what thou hast seen, and the things that are, and the things that are about to be after these" (JND Trans.). The Revelation therefore has a threefold division: First, "what thou hast seen," covered by the glorious vision described in chapter 1 concerning the Son of Man; the second, "the things that are," recorded in chapters 2 and 3, giving a spiritual or prophetic history of the Church during the present age; third, "the things which shall be hereafter," found from chapter 4 to the end of the book.

Therefore, between the end of chapter 3 and the commencement of the heavenly glories revealed in chapter 4, we can safely assume on the authority of Scripture that the saints of this age will have been raptured to be "forever with the Lord" before the "hour of trial" (Rev. 3:10) comes upon the whole world. The following Scriptures reveal this event: John 14:1-3; 1 Corinthians 15:51-52; 1 Thessalonians 1:10; 4:13-18; 5:1-10—all implying the translation of the saints before the judgments of God commence. How it is vividly illustrated by John's own translation in the vision, to heaven, a voice commanding him, "Come up hither." From heaven, John then sees all the unfolding of heaven's glory and God's wrath poured on the earth, even as the glorified saints shall also (Rev. 4:1-2).

The fourth and fifth chapters particularly reveal for our blessing and encouragement, the glories of heaven that shall meet our eyes when we have been raptured to glory at the coming of the Lord for His saints. What John saw in the Apocalyptic vision we shall see! The glories of heaven shall begin unfolding themselves to our wondering eyes as soon as we are there! But let us seek to enjoy a sweet foretaste of them by the help of the Spirit of God (1 Cor. 2:9-10), as we meditate together upon God's precious Word.

THE GLORY OF THE THRONE

The immediate glory reaching our gaze as we enter this heavenly scene is the glory of the throne: "Behold, a throne was set in heaven" (4:2). It is the throne of the Eternal, "high and lifted up" (Isa. 6:1), undoubtedly the highest pinnacle of the universe of God. It stands firm, immovable, and secure, for the attacks of Satanic hosts and evil men cannot move this throne. When the kingdoms of earth are shaken, God's throne and kingdom stand firm. "Wherefore, we receiving a kingdom which cannot be moved, let us have grace, whereby we may serve God acceptably with reverence and godly fear" (Heb. 12:28).

This glorious throne is occupied by One that "to look upon was like a jasper and a sardine (sardius) stone." This limited description of the Occupant implies the impossibility of human intelligence to define the glory of God. Even the Apostle Paul wrote that he was caught up into paradise, and "heard unspeakable things said, which it is not allowed to man to utter" (2 Cor. 12:4; JND Trans.). The jasper is a precious stone, crystalline and purple in color, perhaps a symbol of the glorious rule of God; and the sardius, of fiery red appearance, is perhaps the symbol of divine justice and punitive righteousness which God is about to pour out from heaven to the earth. His infinite glory and judicial wrath are both connected with His throne in the book of Revelation.

Yet surrounding the throne is an emerald rainbow, reminding us that mercy and grace are still divine attributes of God's being, a truth that will never be forgotten through eternity by the redeemed saints, even when they shall gaze upon the glory of God. Even then we shall still sing of His amazing grace.

THE GLORY OF THE ELDERS

Next follows the revelation concerning the glory of the saints: "And round the throne twenty-four thrones, and on the thrones twenty-four elders sitting clothed with white garments; and on their heads golden crowns" (Rev. 4:4). These elders represent the glorified saints in heaven. They are to be clearly distinguished from the living creatures described later.

The following facts indicate the elders represent the glorified saints: i) *they are enthroned,* "sitting," for their pilgrimage below is finished and they are now seated in heavenly glory above; ii) *they are perfected,* "clothed in white garments," fulfilling the eternal purpose of the Father for His children to be "holy and without blame before Him in love" (Eph. 1:4) and that through "the Beloved" alone (Eph. 1:6-7); iii) *they are crowned,* "on their heads golden crowns" (2 Tim. 4:8; 1 Cor. 9:25-27; Rev. 2:10; Phil. 4:1; 1 Pet. 5:3-4). The fact they are crowned indicates that the resurrection and coronation of saints has taken place, another proof that the rapture of saints occurs before the final judgments of God begin; iv) *they worship the Creator.* Though crowned with "golden crowns," yet in perfect humility they acknowledge their personal unworthiness by casting "their crowns before the throne, saying, Thou art worthy, O Lord, to receive glory and honor and power; for Thou hast created all things, and for Thy pleasure they are and were created" (Rev. 4:10-11). God's creatorial glory they perfectly acknowledge in harmony with the "living creatures"; *they worship the Lamb,* "And the four and twenty elders fell down before the Lamb, having every one of them harps, and golden vials full of odors, which are the prayers of saints" (Rev. 5:8). By this action they manifest a living and eternal appreciation of the sufferings of Christ, possessing a sympathetic and affectionate adoration for the Lamb that was slain; vi) *they sing a new song,* "Thou...hast redeemed us to God by Thy blood out of every kindred, and tongue, and people, and nation; and has made us unto our God kings and priests; and we shall reign on the earth." Could any angel or seraph sing this blessed song of redemption? Never! Only the saints who have been redeemed from earth shall ever utter this new song.

"Holy! Holy!" is what the angels sing;
And I expect to help them make the courts of heaven ring!
But when I sing redemption's story they will fold their wings:
For angels never felt the joy that our salvation brings!"

What glory there will be for the saints in that day! His Word will be completed in respect to His purposes for them: "Moreover whom He did predestinate, them He also called; and whom He called, them He also justified; and whom He justified, them He also glorified. What shall we then say to these things? If God be for us, who can be against us?" (Rom. 8:30-31). Let us lay hold of what God has revealed concerning the glory of the saints and lift our hallelujahs to His Throne above even now.

THE GLORY OF THE LIVING CREATURES

Read Revelation 4:6-11. The pavement before the throne is like a crystalline sea, representing the purposes of God, which, contrary to the unprincipled purposes of men (the wicked are like the troubled sea), allow nothing to disturb the tranquillity of His Presence. Four living creatures with a multiplicity of eyes, limitless in discernment, may be viewed as forming the Throne or supporting it. These mysterious beings are somewhat in character like the cherubim and seraphim, consistently associated with the judicial authority of God's throne.

"The cherubim in the temple," writes J. N. Darby in his *Synopsis*, "had two wings, which formed the throne; they looked on the covenant, and at the same time, as of pure gold, were characterized by the divine righteousness of the throne to be approached. In Ezekiel 1, they were the support of the firmament above which the God of Israel was; it was a throne of executory judgment. They had four wings; two to fly with, two to cover themselves. In Ezekiel 10, it appears they were full of eyes (it is not said within) to govern what was outside according to God, not divine intelligence within. In Isaiah 6, the seraphim (or burners) have six wings; they are above the throne, and cry (as in Rev. 4), Holy, Holy, Holy!"

These living creatures with the likeness of man, cattle, beast of the field and fowl of the air, symbolize the intelligence, firmness, power, and rapidity of execution belonging to God in the day of judgment. Yet the heathen know not that God, but rather worship these four species of creation, which are but symbols of His justice! Thus we see the living creatures are connected with the Throne, declaring, defending, and maintaining its holiness, supporting God's universal claim as the Supreme ruler of the Universe. We shall fully comprehend their glory when *in* glory!

THE GLORY OF THE LAMB

The greatest glory of heaven is revealed in chapter 5, for the central object of divine honor and universal adoration is the Lamb. The context reveals that in the right hand of God is a scroll, covered with writing and sealed with seven seals. The subsequent chapters of Revelation indicate the book contains God's counsels and purposes concerning the earth; His judicial actions to be executed and His eternal purposes consummated.

The celestial, terrestrial, and infernal realms of the universe are challenged by a strong angel, calling for one worthy to open the book and loose the seals. When sufficient time elapses, proving that these realms cannot produce the worthy one, John commences to weep, but is immediately comforted by the elder saying, "Weep not, behold the Lion of the tribe of Juda, the Root of David, hath prevailed to open the book, and to loose the seven seals thereof."

As John beholds, it is no richly clad monarch that he sees, but a little lamb with marks of sacrifice upon Him, "a Lamb as it had been slain." Here is the mighty conqueror who alone is worthy to open the book—a little Lamb! How paradoxical! The Lion is the Lamb and the Lamb is a Lion. Twenty-nine times is the expression "the Lamb" (meaning in the original "a little Lamb") used in the Revelation. It suggests the apparent weakness of the once crucified Man of Calvary in contrast to His coming triumph. The once lowly and despised Man of Calvary is the mighty Victor of the Universe. Through death, humiliation, and shame (Phil. 2:5-8), He has proved Himself to be the worthy One appointed as the executor of God's judgments (Jn. 5:22).

With the marks of Calvary eternally His, in the midst of heaven's throng, the Lamb approaches the throne. Upon receiving the book from the Eternal One, the throne's occupant, the Lamb becomes the immediate object of universal acclaim. The first movement of adoration is on the part of the "living creatures" as they fall before "the Lamb." Simultaneously the twenty-four elders do the same, though differing from the "living creatures" through the fact that every one of them have harps, and golden vials full of odors, which are the prayers of saints (Rev. 5:8).

The glorified saints then commence their new song (vv. 9-10)—a song that will re-echo through the endless ages of the coming new creation. How blest will be the song to the heart of the Lamb. He will hear us sing in perfect affection and devotion to Himself, "Thou art worthy to take the book, and to open the seals thereof; for Thou wast slain, and hast redeemed us to God by Thy blood out of every kindred, and tongue, and people, and nation. And has made us unto our God kings and priests; and we shall reign on the earth!" But that is not all!

The myriads of angels around the throne lift up their refrain, saying with a loud voice their sevenfold doxology, surpassing all their previous praises concerning Christ, "Worthy is the Lamb that was slain to receive power, and riches, and wisdom, and strength, and honor, and glory, and blessing" (v. 12). Yet still it is not all, for the universe echoes the worthiness of the Lamb: "Every creature which is in heaven, and on the earth, and under the earth, and such as are in the sea, and all that are in them, heard I saying, Blessing, and honor, and glory, and power, be unto Him that sitteth upon the throne, and unto the Lamb for ever and ever" (v. 13). Every sphere, celestial, terrestrial, and infernal, will acknowledge the Lamb (Phil. 2:9-11). The universe is to be laid at His blessed feet! He alone is worthy.

Is it to be wondered that "the four living creatures said Amen! and the four and twenty elders (glorified saints) fell down and worshipped Him that liveth for ever and ever (v. 14)? Truly the greatest glory in heaven shall ever be the Lamb!

> *"Lord, we own, with hearts adoring,*
> *Thou hast loved us unto blood:*
> *Glory, glory everlasting*
> *Be to Thee, Thou Lamb of God!"*

Part Three
Love's Sweet Secret

25
Three Great Landmarks of His Love

"Remove not the ancient landmarks which thy fathers have set"
(Proverbs 22:28).
"Thus saith the Lord, Stand ye in the ways, and see, and ask for the old paths, where is the good way, and walk therein, and ye shall find rest for your souls. But they said, We will not walk therein"
(Jeremiah 6:16).

God's landmarks and the old paths are still guiding posts for the closing days of Christianity. Laodicean failure prevails around us as foretold by the Lord (Rev. 3:16-17), but His "landmarks" still stand sure in the midst of the failure. His love has provided them to keep us on the path of safety and blessing.

Let me present to you three great landmarks of Christianity which are typified in Numbers 21, by the wilderness experiences of Israel: the brazen serpent on the pole (vv. 4-9), a type of the cross and the death of our Saviour (see Jn. 3:14-15); the springing well, (vv. 16-18), a type of the Holy Spirit of God and His ministry during our age (see Jn. 4:14; 7:37-39); and the tents of Israel pitched "toward the sunrising (vv. 10-11), a type of the coming of the Lord (see Mal. 4:2).

The doctrine of the cross, the doctrine of the Holy Spirit, and the doctrine of the coming of the Lord are three great landmarks given to us by God for our safety and blessing.

1. *The doctrine of the cross:* This is the first "landmark" for Christianity, upon which our faith rests securely. Consider the meaning of the brazen serpent, a type of the cross.

a) The cross is the righteous basis of God's justification of the sinner. This is the great doctrinal teaching of Romans 1-5:11. Note the heart of it in Romans 3:20-26. No one is justified before God and declared righteous apart from the atoning death of Christ on the cross. How many preach this in Christendom today?

b) The cross is the basis of God's sanctification for the saint. This is the great doctrinal teaching of Romans 5:12-8:39, revealing God's way of deliverance for the believer from the power of indwelling sin (Rom. 6:1-11) and the ultimate deliverance from the presence of sin (Rom. 8:18-25). This aspect of the cross many believers fail to manifest in their lives, though delivered from the penalty of their sin (Rom. 3:24; Rom. 5:1). Their walk does not testify: "I am crucified with Christ" (Gal. 2:20).

Paul declared: that the world around me is dead (Gal. 6:14); the world within me is dead (Rom. 6:6-11); the world beneath me is conquered (Col. 2:10-15)—that world ruled by Satan and his hosts (Eph. 6:12); the world above me is now my portion (Eph. 1:3; Col. 3:1-3). How many of us are today anchored to this "landmark" in our daily experience?

c) The cross is the foundation of the Body of Christ. This is the great doctrinal teaching of Ephesians, presenting the truth of the one Body, not many bodies which we see in Christendom. It declares that all believers form the one Body (Eph. 2:8-22). How many Christians today meet together on the ground of this one Body, refusing to be identified with the divisive bodies of Christendom? (See Eph. 4:1-6.)

2. *The doctrine of the Holy Spirit:* This is typified by the springing well. The great landmark of the Spirit was promised by the Saviour (Jn. 14:16-17; 15:26; 16:7-15). His ministry to the Church was established on earth at Pentecost (Acts 2:1-4; 1 Cor. 12:13) and is still existing today. Next to the doctrine of Christ in importance is the doctrine of the Holy Spirit. He is the chief Agent of God and Christ on earth today.

He came with a twofold mission. First, He came on a mission towards the world of convicting and converting (Jn. 16:8-11). Then He also came on a mission towards the Church, to glorify Christ and teach the saints (Jn. 16:12-15). The Book of Acts reveals Him performing that mission, converting souls and gathering them together into corporate companies of local churches. His ministry of guiding "into all truth" (Jn. 16:13) is indicated by the completion of the Word of God.

We, on the other hand, have a twofold responsibility toward the Holy Spirit. First, there is an individual one to yield ourselves to His authority and control (Rom. 12:1-2; 1 Cor. 6:19-20). This will produce "the fruit of the Spirit" in us daily, which is God's desire according to Galatians 5:22-23. Secondly, there is a corporate responsibility to gather with saints who carry out the Word of God in a local testimony, where we seek to assert and maintain the sovereign rights of the Holy Spirit for the energy of our worship and ministry within the assembly. (See 1 Cor. 12). William Kelly has stated, "The presence and operation of the Holy Spirit is the power of the assembly."

Are we faithful to this great landmark of Christianity today? Are we individually under His control and guidance? Are we collectively gathered with like-minded believers who seek to carry out God's truth in corporate character? Note carefully 1 Timothy 3:15.

3. *The doctrine of the coming of the Lord:* This is typified by Israel pitching their tents in the wilderness "toward the sunrising" (Num. 21:10-11). Like Israel, we are also traveling through a barren wilderness toward our home in glory. We are to be "strangers and pilgrims" here according to God's Word (1 Pet. 2:11). The doctrine of the coming of the Lord has been given to us for our encouragement, comfort, strength, and hope, to cheer our hearts in the midst of a desert scene. We have nothing down here to retain; our all is where our Saviour is, in heavenly glory above.

> *"This world is a wilderness wide!*
> *We have nothing to seek or to choose;*
> *We've no thought in the waste to abide,*
> *We've naught to regret nor to lose."* (J. N. Darby)

a) The believers of the early church pitched their tents "toward the sunrising" in light of the truth of the coming of the Lord. His return was imminent to their hearts and it impelled them to live for His glory with great power and blessing. They never lost sight of this landmark of Christianity. The Spirit of God kept it always before them through His servants. (For overwhelming evidence of this, see Rom. 8:24-25, 1 Cor. 1:7; 15:51-58; Phil. 3:20-21; 1 Thess. l:9-10; 4:13-18; 2 Tim. 4:1; Heb. 9:28; Jas. 5:7; 1 Pet. 1:3-5; 2 Pet. 1:10-11; 3:3-9 1 Jn. 3:2-3; Jude 21; Rev. 1:7; and many other Scriptures.)

b) Since then, many believers have moved away from this landmark, neglecting its blessed stabilizing truth. Like "just Lot" (2 Pet. 2:7-8), who pitched his tent toward Sodom (Gen. 13:12), they have set their affections and interests on this present world, rather than toward heaven and the coming of their Lord!

Lot was occupied with a city that was doomed, that went down in destruction. He himself was saved but "as by fire" (1 Cor. 3:15)—yet Sodom perished. This present world under Satan and his godless followers is going down! The believer should not be occupied with a world that is going down, but with what is coming up! "The Sun of righteousness [shall] arise with healing in His wings" (Mal. 4:2). We are not to be occupied with a sunset that will bring the darkest night in human history! We are to be occupied with a coming Sonrise. Are we? Which direction is your tent "pitched," my dear fellow Christian? Where are you in relation to this great landmark? Does your heart now sing:

> *"Sunrise tomorrow! Sunrise tomorrow!*
> *Sunrise in glory is waiting for me.*
> *Sunrise tomorrow! Sunrise tomorrow!*
> *Sunrise with Jesus for eternity!"*

26
The Direction of the Heart

Paul's prayer for his beloved converts is as essential today as when he wrote to them: "The Lord direct your hearts into the love of God and into the patient waiting for Christ" (2 Thess. 3:5). Conditions in the world and in Christendom, with their inherent spiritual dangers, necessitate that our hearts be encouraged in the same direction.

Who directs our hearts? The answer is "the Lord." This title throughout the Thessalonian epistles refers to the Lord Jesus and involves the believer's submission to His authority. "In all thy ways acknowledge Him and He shall direct thy paths" (Prov. 3:6).

Where are we directed? To God and Christ! First, "into the love of God." Three interpretations may be possible. First, that we might learn to love God. In "the last days," we are told that "men shall be lovers of their own selves"; also, "lovers of pleasures more than lovers of God" (2 Tim. 3:1-5). The words of the Scripture in Matthew 22:37 should search our hearts.

Second, that we might apprehend the love of God toward us. (See Eph. 3:19.) Our apprehension of the Father's love should be constantly increasing. (Read Jn. 16:27; Jn. 17:23-26.) Note the precious words of Jesus to His Father concerning us: "...Thou...hast loved them, as Thou hast loved Me." What manner of love this is (1 Jn. 3:1)!

Third, that we might love each other, and all men, after the pattern of God's love. (See Jn. 13:34; 1 Thess. 3:12; 2 Pet. 1:7.) Love is the characteristic word of Christianity. The comprehensiveness of the word "love" is designed to include every aspect of God's love and every possible effect of His love upon the believer. May the Lord direct our hearts!

We are also directed "into the patience of Christ." Three possible interpretations may be taken here also. First, as in the Authorized Version, "into the patient waiting for Christ." We are "to serve the living and true God and to wait for His Son from heaven" (1 Thess. 1:9-10). The word "wait" is also found in Acts 1:4, and the thought of patience is prominent in both Scriptures.

Second, that we should be patient in our suffering as Christ was in His (Heb. 12:2). Peter has written, "If ye do well and suffer...take it patiently; this is acceptable with God" (read 1 Pet. 2:19-21).

Third, since Christ is waiting and expecting His enemies to be made His footstool (Ps. 110:1; Heb. 10:13), the day of His triumph and glory, so we should be patient, knowing that our hope is bound with His and we shall share His glory with Him (Col. 3:4).

We could paraphrase our text by saying, "The Lord teach and make you to love as God loves, and to be patient as Christ is patient." Surely, we all confess the need of such love and patience. And what a wonderful Teacher we have!

> "O patient, spotless One!
> Our hearts in meekness train,
> To bear Thy yoke and learn of Thee,
> That we may rest obtain.
>
> Jesus! Thou art enough
> The mind and heart to fill;
> Thy patient life—to calm the soul;
> Thy love its fear dispel."

27
John's School of Discipleship

Have you enrolled in John's school of discipleship? He was continually controlled by his enjoyment of Christ's love for him, not his love for Christ (read Jn. 13:1; 13:23; 19:25-27; 20:2-4; 21:7, 20). Discipleship is a matter of the heart first, not the head. It begins with the heart at conversion (Rom. 10:9-10). It continues with the heart - Psalm 27:8; Prov. 4:23. It worked for John.

1. *It was the source of spiritual nearness to Christ* (Jn. 13:23-26). He claimed to be one of the disciples whom Jesus loved, but came nearer to Jesus' bosom than others. Peter was not near enough and requested John to ask the Lord his question. The word "lying" in the Greek Text implies that John drew closer to Christ. Do you ever feel near enough to the Lord? Why do we not draw closer, for He loves us! (Jn. 13:1). We can learn the secrets of His heart!

2. *It was the source of spiritual strength* (Jn. 19:25-27). John was the only apostle that stood by the Cross in company with the women. When all the world had rejected the Holy Sufferer, John stayed to the end (Jn. 19:35), sharing His reproach. Can you and I stand alone against the whole world with our rejected Lord? Only His love can enable us to do this! It did for Paul—Gal. 6:14.

3. *It was the source of spiritual progress* (Jn. 20:2-4). Why did John outrun Peter to the empty tomb? Was it the deep consciousness of the love of Christ that impelled him? Was it the lack of it that caused Peter to be slower because he had denied his Lord? Yes, he knew the Lord and boasted that he loved Him. "Knowledge puffeth up, but love edifieth" (1 Cor. 8:1). To the

Galatian believers, Paul wrote, "Ye did run well, who did hinder you?" (5:7). Their vaunted superior knowledge implanted by false teachers affected their hearts. We make little or no spiritual progress when we fail to enjoy the love of Christ.

4. *It was the source of spiritual perception* (Jn. 21:7). In the early morning mist, out of the seven disciples in the boat, it was only John who recognized the voice of the Lord and distinguished His blessed Person. "The disciple whom Jesus loved" had deeper perception and clearer vision than the others! His revelation, "It is the Lord," gave spiritual impetus to Peter at once as he "cast himself into the sea" toward the Master he loved. How much we need disciples today like John, who can reveal the Person of Christ to our hearts.

5. *It was the source of spiritual obedience* (Jn. 21:20-23). Peter, though restored, turned about to see John—"the disciple whom Jesus loved"—following. Because he was curious about John's future path, the Lord virtually says to Peter, "None of your business; follow thou Me." The disciple who enjoyed in his heart the love of Jesus had no need of the admonition, "Follow Me." He followed without being commanded, so dear was the Lord's love to him. Also, Jesus may have intimated that if John lived until the Saviour returned back to earth, John would still be following Him! Is this true of us today?

Why not enroll in John's school of discipleship? Registration fee is a heart that enjoys the love of Christ. The textbook is your Bible where you learn more of His love. Paul knew this, for "the love of Christ" to him was inseparable (Rom. 8:35) impelling (2 Cor. 5:14) and infinite (Eph. 3:19). This technological, sophisticated world can rob us of that simplicity of heart that should be enjoying the love of Christ.

> *"Then fill me, O my Saviour, with Thy love!*
> *Lead, lead me to the living fount above;*
> *Thither may I, in simple faith draw nigh,*
> *And never to another fountain fly,*
> *But unto Thee."* (M. Shekleton)

28
Our Highest Occupation

In John 4:14-24, the Lord discusses the important subject of our worship, revealing the Father's delight when He receives it from us. It is the highest occupation we can engage in, the nearest thing on earth to our employment in heaven (see Rev. 5:8-10). When we gather at the Memorial Feast of the Lord's Supper, do we understand the meaning and character of worship? A word of only seven letters, but seven millenniums can never exhaust its meaning. It is for the Father's heart and the glory of His Son.

What is worship in its true meaning? First consider what it is not. It is not prayer, though allied with it. In prayer, we are occupied with our need, but in worship we are to be wholly occupied with the Person who meets the need. Neither is it ministry, although true ministry should lead us to worship. In ministry, God speaks to us, but in worship we address God. Today it is sometimes evident in our worship gatherings that more ministry is given than worship to God above.

True worship has God for its object; Christ for its subject; the Holy Spirit as its power. It is spontaneous adoration of the soul that sees Christ revealed by the Spirit of God. To worship acceptably, two requirements should be noted: a purged conscience and a full heart (Heb. 10:22). The first is the result of the blood of Christ; the second is the result of heart occupation with the Person of Christ. True worship is adoration of the heart and may or may not be expressed in words (Lk. 7:37-38; Jn. 12:1-3).

Where do we worship? In John 4:20-22, the Lord indicates that there is no earthly locality where we worship in this dispensation; not at Jerusalem or elsewhere. The true place of worship is in heaven, "the holiest of all" (Heb. 10:19). There we are invited to enter "within the veil" and worship God in His holy presence. As to our bodies, we are on earth, but in spirit we worship in heaven. Our earthly gathering place is sanctified by the presence of our Lord Himself (Mt. 18:20). With Him we enter "the holiest" in the Spirit, and it is He who leads the praise and worship of His people. (See Ps. 22:22; Heb. 2:12).

How do we worship? "God is a Spirit: and they that worship Him must worship Him in spirit and in truth" (Jn. 4:24). The Spirit of God is the power for worship and the Word of God the only guide for worshipping the true God. The holy anointing oil was first placed on the blood-sprinkled ear, hand, and foot of the priest before he entered the sanctuary of God as a worshipper (Lev. 8:30). The anointing oil is a type of the Holy Spirit, who is still the power, whether for conflict, service, or worship.

The supreme Object of worship: "The Father seeketh worshippers," said Jesus (Jn. 4:23). When the priests of old laid the parts of the sacrifice on the altar of burnt offering, they watched it ascend as a sweet savor to Jehovah (Lev. 1:10-12). So in the Memorial Feast of the Lord's Supper, we see Christ giving Himself for us "an offering and a sacrifice to God for a sweet smelling savor" (Eph. 5:2). This touches our hearts as nothing else can, drawing from us worship to the Father for the unspeakable Gift of His beloved Son. Thus we share fellowship with the Father in His thoughts and His appreciation of His Son, as the Holy Spirit unfolds to us more of the excellencies of Christ, of whom it is written: "No man knoweth the Son, but the Father" (Mt. 11:27). In this manner, our worship rises to the Father's heart to delight Him above!

The eternal duration of worship: In the day of eternal glory, the new heavens and the new earth will be one vast sanctuary, when the whole redeemed creation will form one united choir, ascribing glory and worship to God (Eph. 3:21). The universal song will be: "Blessing, and honor, and glory, and power, be unto Him that sitteth upon the throne, and unto the Lamb for ever and ever" (Rev. 5:13). Until then, may we know the meaning of true worship here below, for it is our highest occupation!

29
The Bath, the Bason & the Bosom

Meditation on the Lord's ministry in John 13 takes us into the Upper Room of God's rich blessing; there we discover the precious truths which His actions illustrate:

1. *The Bath—the judicial cleansing of the soul:* "Jesus says to him, he that is washed all over, needs not to wash save his feet, but is wholly clean" (Jn. 13:10, JND). The context reveals that Peter, after being told he would have no part with the Lord unless his feet were washed, ardently demands to be washed from head to foot. The Lord declared that he was "wholly clean," and needed only his feet washed. Notice John 15:3, where the Lord said to them, "Now ye are clean through the word which I have spoken unto you." The disciples (except Judas) had received the judicial cleansing of their souls through repentance and faith in the Lord. This is the bath the sinner needs. How did we receive this?

Read Revelation 1:5; 5:9; 7:14. It is only through the precious blood of Christ, as Peter also declares in 1 Peter 1:18-19. John agrees in 1 John 1:7; and many other Scriptures add corroborating proof. That one bath is satisfactory to God forever. "For by one offering He hath perfected forever them that are sanctified" (Heb. 10:14). Do you remember the time you had this bath?

2. *The Bason: moral cleansing from daily defilement.* "He poureth water into a bason, and began to wash the disciples' feet" (Jn. 13:5). The ministry of "the bason" was for their feet. The "water" typifies the Word of God that cleanses our walk through this defiled world. Ephesians 5:25-26 shows the Lord's provision for keeping His Church "sanctified" and "cleansed" until He

returns "with the washing of water by the Word." The Psalmist wrote, "Wherewithal shall a young man cleanse his way? by taking heed thereto according to Thy Word" (Ps. 119:9). Without this ministry, collectively or individually, our walk down here would not be in fellowship with Him (see Jn. 13:8).

Look at the priest in the Old Testament; when instituted to the office, he was given a ceremonial bath (Ex. 29:4; Lev. 8:6) and only once. Yet, when serving Jehovah in connection with the tabernacle ministry, he must wash his hands and feet before each act of service (Ex. 30:17-21). What a blessed type for us! One bath but always using the laver of the Word of God. Saint, do not neglect the bason. The risen Lord still uses this to wash our feet and to wipe them gently with a towel. Is it not written: "He will keep the feet of His saints" (1 Sam. 2:9).

3. *The Bosom: the divine purpose.* This is the goal—to reach the bosom of Christ! "Now there was leaning on Jesus' bosom, one of His disciples whom Jesus loved" (Jn. 13:23). Is not this where the ministry of the bason will bring us? This One was sent from the "bosom of the Father" (Jn. 1:18) in order that we may lean on the bosom of His Son! John knew this above the others, proved it and enjoyed it. He boasts not of his love for Jesus, but the love of Jesus for him! There is room for you, and me on His bosom.

There we find rest (Ps. 37:7; Mt. 11:28-30); rest for heart and mind; from heartaches and trials. Also safety, for it is the bosom of divine omnipotence. Upon God alone O my soul, rest peacefully (Ps. 62:5; Song of Sol. 8:5; Ps. 23:4). There we find knowledge. John alone was near to Jesus to ask Peter's question (Jn. 13:23-25; Deut. 29:29; 1 Cor. 2:15). Upon His breast we learn His secrets. Best of all, we find His love. John's secret nearness was knowing how much Jesus loved him. Are you finding out His love? Rejoice in your bath, and use the bason to get to the bosom. It will support you all the way home to glory, until we see His face. Let our prayer be:

> "Nearer! Still nearer! Close to Thy heart,
> Draw me, my Saviour, so precious Thou art;
> Fold me, oh, fold me, close to Thy breast,
> Shelter me safe in that haven of rest!"

Scripture Index

GENESIS		29:29	122	JOB	
1:2	88	33:12	5	14:1-2	14
2:21-3:7	95	JOSHUA		PSALMS	
3:17-19	89	4:18	49	2:6	99
5:22	38	4:19-20	47	2:8-9	42
5:23	37	5:2-11	47	2:9	70
5:24	81	6	48	2:10-12	70
6:3	37	JUDGES		16:11	53
12:8	41	16	44	17:15	77
12:10	41	1 SAMUEL		17:15	80
13	42	2:9	122	18:9-12	91
13:3	41	2 SAMUEL		22:22	120
13:10	42	11:1	45	23	57
13:12	42	11:1-5	44	23	62
13:12	114	12:23	79	23:4	59
19:1, 6-7	42	19:10	101	23:4	122
20:2	41	23:10	24	24	100
26:7	42	1 KINGS		27:8	117
28:10-22	47	12:28-33	48	37:7	122
28:13-15	48	16:34	48	39:4-5	13
EXODUS		22:4	45	40:3	17
3:7	87	2 KINGS		46:6, 10	55
13:21	91	2:1-14	47	51	45
14:13-14	56	2:4-6	48	55:6	37
15:1-6	70	2:9-11	82	55:22	69
25:13-15	79	2:11	49	62:5	57
29:4	122	3:6-7	46	62:5	122
30:17-21	122	6:8-23	81	62:10	28
40:34-38	91	9:30-37	49	72:9	42
LEVITICUS		1 CHRONICLES		84:4	20
1:10-12	120	16:35	17	90:9	13
8:6	122	16:35	19	110:1	75
8:30	120	29:15	13	110:1	116
NUMBERS		2 CHRONICLES		110:3	79
12-14	43	5:1-9	79	110:5-6	70
12:3	22	18	45	119:9	122
16	74	18	49	119:11	18
21	111	19:1-2	46	138:8	79
21:10-11	113	20	56	139:23-24	43
21:16-18	33	20:15	70	PROVERBS	
DEUTERONOMY		NEHEMIAH		3:5-6	24
29:29	81	8:10	52	3:6	115

4:23	117	6:16	111	24:4-8	72
22:28	111	30:7	93	24:30	91
23:23	29	**Ezekiel**		24:32-33	71
Ecclesiastes		1	106	24:36-44	71
10:1	43	10	106	24:39	37
Song of Songs		**Daniel**		25:31-46	92
2:10	96	2:40-44	72	27:1-53	82
8:5	122	2:44-45	93	**Mark**	
Isaiah		7:13	92	1:35	57
6	106	7:13-14	99	8:35	15
6:1	104	7:18	97	13:26	91
7:14	100	7:23-28	72	**Luke**	
9:6	100	10:5-7	82	2:25-35	51
11:5	100	**Amos**		2:36-38	52
11:6-9	89	3:3	38	4:1-13	23
12:6	100	**Habakkuk**		4:13	24
22:21-25	69		1-3	6:12-13	58
24:21	97		25-26	7:37-38	119
26:3	24	**Zechariah**		12:32	97
28:16	69	10:4	69	12:35-37	74
30:15-16	57	12:1-14	93	16:19-31	79
30:7	57	13:1-6	93	24:15-16	83
32:1	101	14:1-3	70	24:31	83
32:1-2	99	14:9	99	**John**	
33:17	100	**Malachi**		1:18	122
33:22	70	4:2	77	3:14-15	111
33:22	100	4:2	111	3:36	31
33:24	101	4:2	114	4:14	35
35:1-2	89	**Matthew**		4:14	111
37:36	70	1:21	75	4:14-24	119
40:6-7	14	1:23	100	4:23	20
40:10-11	98	5-7	100	4:23-24	120
42:1	100	6:10	99	5:22	107
42:4	100	7:13-14	53	5:24	17
44:6	100	8:11	79	5:24	31
50:4	57	11:27	120	6:37	94
51:21-23	93	11:28	94	7:37-39	111
53	93	11:28-30	122	10:28	31
53:6	69	13:41-42	93	12:1-3	119
53:7	22	16:18	69	13	121
53:11	95	17:1-8	82	13:1	117
55:13	89	17:3	79	13:5	121
61:2-3	93	18:20	31	13:8	122
63	70	18:20	120	13:10	121
64:6	51	21:42	69	13:23	122
65:25	89	22:37	115	13:23-25	122
Jeremiah		24; 25	72	13:23-26	117

Scripture Index

13:34	115	1-8	87	5:11, 13	32
14:1-3	32	3:20-26	112	6:2	97
14:1-3	103	5:1	112	6:19-20	113
14:3	85	5:5	22	8:1	117
14:16-17	112	5:12-8:39	112	9:24-27	80
14:21	39	6:1-11	112	9:24-27	66
14:23	39	6:6-11	112	9:25-27	22
14:27	22	6:23	17	9:25-27	105
14:27	24	7:18	66	10:11	33
15:3	121	7:24-25	66	10:11	38
15:11	22	8	18	10:11	41
15:18-19	46	8:18	87	10:11	44
15:19	32	8:18-25	112	10:12	28
15:26	112	8:19-21	89	12	113
16:7-15	112	8:22-27	88	12:13	18
16:8-11	112	8:23	79	12:13	32
16:12-15	112	8:23	84	12:13	112
16:13	113	8:23	89	13:4	22
16:13-14	96	8:23-25	18	13:12	79
16:27	115	8:24-25	114	15:1-4	31
16:33	66	8:28	89	15:23	86
16:33	70	8:29-30	89	15:24-28	98
17:15-17	19	8:30-31	106	15:43	96
17:23-26	115	8:31	90	15:44-46	84
19:25-27	117	8:34-35	90	15:49	84
19:35	117	8:35	118	15:51, 53	84
20:2-4	117	8:37	70	15:51-52	103
20:14-15	83	10:9-10	117	15:51-54	32
21:7	117	12:1-2	21	15:51-58	85
21:7	118	12:1-2	35	15:51-58	114
21:20	117	12:1-2	113	15:52	86
21:20-23	118	13:11-12	89	**2 Corinthians**	
Acts		15:4	18	3:2-3	22
1:4	116	15:4	38	4:15-18	15
1:11	32	**1 Corinthians**		4:16	66
2:1-4	112	1:2	31	5:1, 4	14
2:30	26	1:7	114	5:2, 4	84
3:20-21	98	1:12	31	5:9	39
4:11	69	1:21	28	5:10	22
7:44-60	82	2:9	81	5:14	118
9:1-7	83	2:9-10	104	6:14-16	46
10:38	22	2:14	81	6:14-17	19
10:40-41	83	2:15	122	6:14-18	32
20:27	67	3:15	114	6:18-7:1	19
27:21	30	4:2	22	10:3-5	66
Romans		4:3-5	68	10:3-5	23
1-5:11	112	4:17	22	12:1-4	83

12:4	104	5:32	95	5:1-10	103
GALATIANS		6:10-18	23	5:3	93
1:9	31	6:10-18	66	5:3-4	71
2:20	66	6:12	23	5:5-6	77
2:20	112	6:12	85	5:6-10	71
4:6	20	6:12	112	2 THESSALONIANS	
5:7	118	PHILIPPIANS		2:1-3	74
5:16-17	21	1:6	79	3:5	115
5:22-23	22	1:21	21	3:6	32
5:22-23	113	1:23-24	65	1 TIMOTHY	
6:10	22	2:5-8	107	1:10	30
6:14	66	2:9-11	108	1:19-20	27
6:14	112	3:10	49	3:15	32
6:14	117	3:13-14	67	3:15	48
EPHESIANS		3:20-21	18	3:15	113
1:3	22	3:20-21	79	3:15-16	27
1:3	112	3:20-21	94	4:1	27
1:4	105	3:20-21	114	4:1-7	73
1:5	89	3:21	84	4:12	23
1:6-7	105	3:21	89	5:8	27
1:7	94	4:1	105	5:11-15	28
1:11	89	4:6-7	24	6:3	30
1:22-23	18	COLOSSIANS		6:9-10	28
1:22-23	32	1:18	95	6:20-21	28
1:23	84	1:25-28	30	2 TIMOTHY	
2:2	23	2:10-15	112	1:12	30
2:2	85	3:1-3	112	1:12	31
2:8-22	112	3:4	116	1:12	68
2:10	18	1 THESSALONIANS		1:13	29
2:13-16	18	1:9-10	114	1:13	30
2:20-21	69	1:9-10	116	1:13	31
3:19	115	1:10	40	1:15	30
3:19	118	1:10	94	2:2	31
3:21	97	1:10	103	2:15	34
3:21	120	2:19-20	79	2:17-18	27
4:1-6	112	2:19-20	80	2:19	69
4:3-6	18	3:12	115	2:20-21	19
4:14-15	30	4:13-18	32	2:20-21	48
4:30	84	4:13-18	77	2:22	19
4:32	22	4:13-18	92	3:1-5	28
5:2	120	4:13-18	103	3:1-5	72
5:25-26	121	4:13-18	114	3:1-5	115
5:25-27	95	4:15-17	40	3:10-12	30
5:27	84	4:15-17	83	3:13	72
5:27	95	4:15-18	50	3:14	31
5:27	96	4:16-17	84	3:14-17	18
5:30	18	4:17	85	3:16-17	31

Scripture Index

3:16-17	34	12:2	116	3:2	79
4:1	92	12:6	45	3:2	94
4:1	114	12:28	104	3:2-3	114
4:2	31	13:12-13	19	5:13	31
4:3	30	13:15	19	5:18	24
4:3-4	74	13:20	59	5:19	71
4:6	65	JAMES		2 JOHN	
4:7-8	66	3	43	:8	80
4:8	67	4:14	14	:8-10	32
4:8	80	5:7	114	JUDE	
4:8	105	5:7-11	22	:3	27
TITUS		5:8	71	:11	73
1:9	30	1 PETER		:14-15	38
1:13	30	1:3-5	18	:14-15	39
2:1	30	1:3-5	114	:14-15	55
2:2	30	1:14-16	22	:14-15	91
2:13	25	1:18-19	121	:14-15	94
2:13	32	2:1-10	32	:21	84
HEBREWS		2:4-8	69	:21	114
1:9	95	2:11	113	:23	37
2:12	120	2:19-21	116	:23	94
2:18	18	2:23	22	REVELATION	
3:12	44	2:24	69	1-5	103
4:9	79	5:3-4	105	1:1	91
4:12	24	5:4	80	1:5	121
4:14-16	18	5:7	69	1:5-6	32
4:14-16	32	2 PETER		1:7	55
7:25	18	1:7	115	1:7	77
7:25	32	1:10-11	114	1:7	91
8:11	80	1:11	97	1:7	114
9:14	17	1:11	98	1:19	103
9:14	60	1:16-18	82	2-3	44
9:28	114	1:19	75	2-3	74
10:13	116	1:21	31	2:10	80
10:14	121	2	73	2:10	105
10:19	32	2:7-8	42	2:28	76
10:19	120	2:7-8	114	3:7	69
10:22	119	3:3-7	93	3:10	103
10:37	25	3:3-9	114	3:11-12	80
11:1	26	3:18	56	3:16-17	111
11:1	35	3:18	80	4	106
11:4	39	1 JOHN		4:1-2	103
11:5	37	1:7	121	4:2	104
11:5-6	38	2:14-17	66	4:4	105
11:5	81	2:15	32	4:6-11	106
11:39	86	2:15-17	19	4:10-11	105
12:1-2	67	3:1	115	5	86

5	107	14:13	52	22:3	80
5:8	105	17:12-14	72	22:3	98
5:8	107	17:16-17	74	22:3-4	85
5:8-10	119	19:6-9	95	22:5	97
5:9	121	19:11	70	22:5	98
5:9-14	108	19:11-21	55	22:7	99
5:10	32	19:11-21	74	22:12	99
5:13	120	20	98	22:16	75
6:16-17	93	20:2-7	97	22:16	77
7	26	20:7-10	98	22:17	85
7:14	121	20:11-15	92	22:20	85
9:20-21	73	20:11-15	98	22:20	86
11:15	99	21	96	22:20	94
13	72	21:1-5	92	22:20	99
13	55	21:3-5	98		